BALTIMORE
BEER

BEER

A Satisfying History of
Charm City Brewing

Rob Kasper

Foreword by Boog Powell ★ Photography by Jim Burger

Published by American Palate
A Division of The History Press
Charleston, SC 29403
www.historypress.net

Copyright © 2012 by Rob Kasper
All rights reserved

Cover images: Front cover image by Jim Burger. Back cover workman courtesy of the Baltimore Museum of Industry, and Globe light of American beer courtesy of the David Donovan Collection, photo by Edward Brown.

First published 2012
Second printing 2012

ISBN 978-1-5402-0656-5

Library of Congress Cataloging-in-Publication Data

Kasper, Rob.
Baltimore beer : a satisfying history of Charm City brewing / Rob Kasper.
p. cm.
Includes bibliographical references and index.
ISBN 978-1-5402-0656-5
1. Beer industry--Maryland--Baltimore--History. 2. Brewing industry--Maryland--Baltimore--History. 3. Brewers--Maryland--Baltimore--History. 4. Beer--Maryland--Baltimore--History. I. Title.
HD9397.U53B355 2012
338.4'7663420975271--dc23
2012009491

Notice: The information in this book is true and complete to the best of our knowledge. It is offered without guarantee on the part of the author or The History Press. The author and The History Press disclaim all liability in connection with the use of this book.

All rights reserved. No part of this book may be reproduced or transmitted in any form whatsoever without prior written permission from the publisher except in the case of brief quotations embodied in critical articles and reviews.

Contents

Foreword, by John "Boog" Powell	7
Preface	11
Introduction	17
Early Brewing in Baltimore: Amid the Mud and the Wolves a Town and Its Breweries Are Born	23
National Beer: Glory, Fading and Resurrection	42
Gunther, Globe, Free State and American: The Other Post-Prohibition Breweries	57
Advertising: It's All in the Jingle	70
Sports and Beer	81
Beer and Food	91
Collectors	103
A New Breed of Baltimore Brewers	109
Appendix: Zion Lutheran Church and the Early Baltimore Brewers	139
Timeline of Significant Dates in Baltimore Brewing History	145
Glossary of Basic Beerspeak	149
Bibliography	151
Index	155
About the Author and Photographer	159

Foreword

In addition to baseball and barbecue, I know a little something about beer. It is my beverage of choice and has been for as long as I have been smacking long balls and smoking pork shoulders, and that goes back some years.

I had the honor of opening the first Baltimore Beer Week celebration in 2009, tapping a cask of local craft beer for the thirsty souls gathered on the historic warship the USS *Constellation*, anchored in Baltimore's harbor. The video of my mighty swat even made YouTube.

But around Maryland, people mostly know me either because of my statistics or my sandwiches. My statistics in sixteen years with the Baltimore Orioles, Cleveland Indians and Los Angeles Dodgers—339 career home runs, four All-Star Games, a World Series title in 1966 and American League Most Valuable Player in 1970—are nothing to shake a stick at. My sandwiches—barbecued pit beef, pork and turkey—draw crowds of avid eaters both at my operation beyond the right field wall at Oriole Park in Camden Yards and at my restaurant on the boardwalk in Ocean City, Maryland.

Around the country, most people know me because I appeared in a series of television commercials for Miller Lite Beer. I was one of the twenty-five Lite "All Stars," twenty-four guys plus "The Doll," Lee Meredith, who shot eighty-one commercials from 1973 to 1983 for light beer. The commercials were funny, featuring exaggerated characters like John Madden as a hyper coach and Jim Honochick as an umpire who mistakes the late Bubba Smith, the gigantic and now-deceased Baltimore Colts defensive end, for me, the svelte first baseman for the Orioles. How blind can you be!?

Foreword

Those light beer commercials, which featured two teams—one claiming that the beer "tastes great" and the other that it was "less filling"—caused quite a stir. According to Frank DeFord, a writer who grew up in Baltimore, they were the most popular commercials in the history of television. DeFord might be prejudiced. He appeared in one of the spots, got to keep the brown Harris tweed sports coat he wore during the filming and later wrote a book (*Lite Reading*, Penguin Books, 1984) chronicling the adventures of the Lite Beer All Stars.

I can testify that the world does notice you when you are in a beer commercial. When I was a ballplayer, people I met thought that they might have heard of me. But after the commercials, people not only recognized me, they also felt like they knew me.

Making beer commercials was a whole new second career for me. I was released by the Dodgers in September 1977. Having September off was a new experience for me. One day I was looking at this Miller Lite TV commercial that had Marv Thronberry in it. And I thought if Marv can do that, I can do that. So I called up my agent, Marty Blackman, and said, "Marty, I want to do one of those Miller commercials." He checked into it and found out that I would have to audition for a part. So I went up to New York, and they looked at me, and they said, "We will let you know." A week later, they called me and said, "You got it."

The first commercial I did was with umpire Jim Honochick—the one where he doesn't realize who he is talking to until he puts on his glasses and says, "Hey, you're Boog Powell." It was pretty neat. It was the first time anybody had publicly poked fun at an umpire. I had no idea that thirteen years later I would still be doing them. I did seventeen total, including a few with former Green Bay Packers running back Paul Horning and three with Koichi Numazawa, a Japanese ballplayer who used to karate chop the card table every time I asked him to "cut the cards."

Not only did I make some good money, I also learned about the beer business as I traveled around the United States, making appearances for Miller Lite. If you can think of the name of a weekend event, I have probably appeared at it.

Typically, I would arrive in town on a Friday and that night have dinner with "selected accounts," folks the local Miller distributor was cozy with. On Saturday, I would go the public event, whether it was a volleyball tournament or a chili contest, I was there. On Saturday night, I would go with the distributor to visit restaurants, bars and mom-and-pops and talk to the owners. That kind of personal contact was an invaluable tool to the salesmen, who were trying to get this establishment to put their beer on tap. I learned a lot about the beer business, and for a time, I thought I might get

Foreword

a Miller Lite distributorship. But it didn't happen. I was comfortable talking to people about beer, and I was pretty good at it.

I wasn't born in Baltimore, but I feel like I grew up here. Let's say I did my graduate work here—Eating Crabs and Drinking Beer 101. When Jerry Hoffberger owned the Orioles, he also owned National Brewing Company. This meant that at the beginning of every home stand, there would be a couple of cases of free beer in your locker. A few guys didn't drink, so I would offer to relieve them of their beer. Sometimes I would collect eight to ten cases per home stand, a good fringe benefit.

A bunch of us—Curt Belfrey, Terry Crowley, Brooks Robinson and I—lived near Memorial Stadium on Medford Road. So, after night games we would get together in somebody's backyard, eat crabs, fix barbecue and drink National Bohemian. Nowadays people treat professional athletes like celebrities, often worshiping the ground they walk on. But back when I played at Memorial Stadium and lived on Medford Road, people treated me like the guy next door. One night, we were going at it pretty late, making noise, and one of my row neighbors hollered out of his window at me: "Hey Powell, you don't have to go to work tomorrow morning, but we do!" We toned it down. What a great neighborhood.

Since Hoffberger owned National, I was loyal to his beers. When I was living in Miami, I drank Regal, just because it was a National Brewing Company Product. Hoffberger was a wonderful man. The first time you met him, you felt like you had known him forever. I was loyal to National, maybe loyal to a fault. But I am still that way today; I am loyal to the locals whether they are brewers or tavern operators.

My memories are one man's story of how life in Baltimore has been affected by its breweries. This book records many more such tales. In words and pictures, it gives an overview of the history of brewing in Baltimore, from the early alehouses along the Jones Falls to the beer gardens that once lined its streets, the spirited sales battles between National and its rivals and the recent appearance of craft brewers. As Baltimore breweries battled for beer drinkers, they painted the town with posters, plastered advertisements on scoreboards and bought space in game programs. They even gave away booklets with tips on how to cook with beer. With the help of local collectors, men who treasure the memorabilia of old Baltimore breweries, this book mines the city's rich, sudsy past and shows its fondness for the brewer's art.

Enjoy the journey through these pages, with or without a cold one.

–John "Boog" Powell

Preface

If this book project were a beer, it would definitely be classified as a vintage issue.

It began more than a decade ago as a book to be published by Woodholme Press, the imprint of the Bibelot Baltimore area bookstores. When Woodholme collapsed in bankruptcy in 2001, the book project lay dormant. Then, in 2011, after close to thirty-five years writing for the *Baltimore Sun*, I said goodbye to the newspaper and took up the book. This book, like a popular Baltimore craft beer, experienced a resurrection.

Many people helped with this project, and high on the list are librarians. I visited the Maryland Room of the Enoch Pratt Library where Jeff Korman and his staff have extensive hanging files on Baltimore institutions. I sat in the inner sanctum, the Mencken Room of the Pratt, and with the assistance of Vincent Fitzpatrick, curator of the H.L. Mencken Collection, saw the scrawling handwriting of the "Sage of Baltimore," discoursing on one of his favorite topics, beer. An excerpt of a Mencken letter was published by permission of the Enoch Pratt Free Library of Baltimore. I trekked to many other area libraries. Tom Beck, chief curator of the Albin O. Kuhn Library at the University of Maryland Baltimore County; Ann Hudak, special collections librarian of the University of Maryland Libraries; Catherine H. Scott at the Baltimore Museum of Industry; Alison P. Kelley of the Science Reference Section of the Library of Congress; Eden Dennis and Francis O'Neill at the Maryland Historical Society; and Paul McCardell of the *Baltimore Sun* library all provided excellent assistance. Online catalogues are terrific, but they are no match for an experienced librarian to tell you what

Preface

is in a collection and how to find it. I would be remiss, however, if I did not give a bow in thanks to the Baltimore County Library and its online archive of Baltimore newspapers. Anyone mining the past of this city will be well served by this treasure of local history.

Baltimore has the reputation of being a big city that behaves like a small town. Talk to anyone in this town for twenty minutes, the theory goes, and you will find out that you have a mutual acquaintance or even a relative. I benefited from this old-fashioned style of social networking. The Hoffberger family, for instance, was well known as one of city's prominent families. Their names are on museums and foundations. I got to know the Hoffbergers on the dusty fields of the Roland Park Baseball League and the sweaty confines of the Towsontowne Basketball League when my sons played on recreational teams with Hoffberger offspring and I was a volunteer coach. Thanks to that experience, Peter Hoffberger and his wife, Lisa, director of communications for the Foundation for Alcohol Research, introduced me to Peter's brother, David, the family historian. David graciously shared his extensive files on his father's tenure as head of the National Brewing Company and the Baltimore Orioles. David, in turn, led me to Howard Cohen, descendant of the family who ran Gunther Brewing Company. He along with his sister, JoAnn Fruchtman, provided me with a trove of Gunther newsletters and personal recollections. Thanks, too, to David Donovan, a collector, who opened his home collection of beer ephemera to me.

National Beer's "Land of Pleasant Living" advertising campaign was a classic, and some of the men familiar with it—Bill Costello, Don Schnably, Herb Fried and Gilbert Sandler—helped me reconstruct the story behind both it, as well as the clever Colt 45 campaign. As Alex Castro's documentary film *Mr. Boh's Brewery* shows so well, the workers at National were a lively bunch, and an interview with Jerry DiPaolo, the former head of brewery sales, showed me that he still had plenty of fire in his nineties. Robert W. Kroeger Jr., a former executive at National Brewing Company, provided perspective on the business of brewing.

David Knipp, of Obrecht Commercial Real Estate, the enterprise that is transforming old breweries on Brewers Hill into commercial and residential uses, provided photos. The Brewers Hill renovation, along with the striking rehabilitation of the American Brewery, now home to Humanim, a nonprofit social services provider, are testimonials both to the past grandeur of Baltimore breweries and to the bright future of the restored buildings.

The Zion Lutheran Church, behind city hall, as the church for many of the city's German brewers, played a central role in the city's early brewing

Preface

history, a role that Mark Duerr, one of the church's unofficial historians, documented and shared. Another valuable resource was the website www.germanmarylanders.org, overseen by Shelly Arnold, that follows the history of the city's prominent Germans, right to their final resting places in Baltimore-area cemeteries.

The city's craft beer community, and in particular Hugh Sisson, Volker Stewart and Bill Oliver, provided both technical knowledge and demonstrated the spirit of curiosity and innovation. Al Spoler's 2010 television documentary *Brewed on the Bay* provided a synopsis of the beer movement in Maryland. The *City Paper* reporting of Brennen Jensen and the blogs of Alexander Mitchell IV, Brad Klipner and Tom Cizauskas provided valuable information.

One of the best things that has happened to the Baltimore beer scene has been the creation of Baltimore Beer Week, an annual October celebration of the city's brewing arts. In 2011, Baltimore Beer Week founders Joe Gold and Dominic Cantalupo led a tour of the city's old brewing sites that helped me to complete this book.

Thanks go out as well to writers Christopher Corbett, Neil Grauer, Richard O'Mara and Fred Rasmussen, all of whom encouraged me; photographers Jim Burger and Edward Brown, who shot endless photos; and Mary Mashburn and Steve St. Angelo at Typecast Press. *Baltimore Sun* publisher Timothy Ryan and top editor Mary Corey graciously permitted the use of some of the newspaper's photos. Thanks, too, go to Gregg Wilhelm, formerly at Woodholme and now head of City Lit, who provided images from the early days of the project, as well as to my collaborator, Turkey Joe Trabert, whose unfailing good humor and countless store of barroom stories kept me going in dry times.

My editor at The History Press, Hannah Cassilly, has been a rock, steering me through the vicissitudes of publishing and maintaining an interest in a book about Baltimore, her hometown.

I am tremendously grateful to my family. My sons, Matthew and Michael, who have long had an interest in drinking their father's beer, have buoyed me with their enthusiasm for this project. As is true with many of my endeavors, I could not have written this book without the help of my wife, Judy. Her assistance in computer matters, her good editorial judgment, her cooking skills and her dogged persistence were invaluable. Some guys get lucky in life, and thanks to her, I am one of them.

The idea for this book was hatched one ordinary May afternoon in 1996. I was reading old newspaper clippings in the downtown offices of the *Baltimore*

Preface

Sun, scrambling to put together a column on the demise of National Premium. As I worked, I was struck by how strong a role breweries had played in city's daily life and by how much of Baltimore's beer history seemed to be slipping away, generation by generation. There ought to be a book, I thought, that concisely told in words and photographs the story of this city and its beers.

Then began a process that had fits and starts and would stretch out for years. I was helped by Joe Trabert. A native of Baltimore, a onetime schoolteacher and now a retired state worker, he is widely known as "Turkey Joe," the name he applied to the Fells Point bar he ran for eight years. His knowledge of the city, his tales and his connections to the community of collectors of Baltimore breweriana were invaluable. Massive breweries once stood in the North Avenue–Gay Street neighborhood called "Brewers Row," while more than thirty dotted east Baltimore, many near the junction of Conkling and O'Donnell Streets known as "Brewers Hill." Collectors like Joe not only knew where the bottles and cans were buried, they could also provide glimpses of what life was like in this once frothy town.

I tracked down men and women who worked in Baltimore's beer business. They, too, had stories to tell. I listened to front-office types like National Brewing Company executive Frank Cashen and to Dawson Farber, who granted me long interviews before he died in 2007. I got the opportunity to talk with Ernie Harwell and Chuck Thompson before they passed. These colorful broadcasters not only had to do play-by-plays of sporting events but also had to pour a perfect-looking beer during commercials. I heard stories from former brewery truck drivers as they met for lunch and at a Teamster's Hall in east Baltimore. These firsthand accounts were mixed with recollections drawn from relatives of Jerry Hoffberger and other prominent players in the city's brewing past. Finally, John Steadman, the departed dean of Baltimore sportswriters and a man with a generous heart and a magnificent memory, provided many colorful stories of days and beers gone by before he left us.

In an effort to put some historical order to the mounds of memorabilia, I turned to *Brewing in Maryland* by William Kelley. This massive, self-published effort came out in 1965 and is now out of print. Reading Kelley's lengthy accounts of the corporate histories of Baltimore breweries from 1703 to 1965 and consulting the timelines set out in *American Breweries II* by Dale P. Van Wieren helped me weave my way through the family tree of Baltimore brewers. Sometimes the foliage was thick, with several families—Bauernschmidts, Wiessners and Von der Horsts—producing several brewers who sometimes worked together and sometimes set up

Preface

competing businesses. It was hard to keep your Bauernschmidts and Wiessners straight without consulting these seminal works.

In this book, I strive to go beyond a dry accounting of who brewed what and when. With words and photographs, I tell the story of this city's rich, sudsy social history. It is a lively tale, starting back in the days of "The Star-Spangled Banner," when alehouses lined the Jones Falls and a seamstress, Mary Pickersgill, sewed Old Glory as the flag was stretched out on a brewery floor.

It tells of the turn-of-the-century Germans who erected elaborate breweries and leafy beer gardens along the Gay Street–North Avenue corridor. It tells of the 1950s and '60s, when Gunther, National, American and Arrow mounted clever advertising campaigns and tried to wrap themselves around the Orioles and the Colts as the breweries battled for the palates and wallets of the Chesapeake Bay's burgeoning beer-drinking population. It finishes up with the stories behind the current crop of local brewpub operators and craft brewers who are putting modern spins on the century-old routine of making beer. After studying this city's past, there is little doubt that Baltimore is a suds city, a town that takes its beer seriously.

Introduction

To fully appreciate the historical role that breweries have had on the city, it is helpful to have an overview of basic brewing procedures and terms. For starters, it is useful to remember that four basic components—water, yeast, grain and hops—go into beer. And you can toss out the water. Baltimore happens to be blessed with good beer-making water, but technology now means that almost any brewery can add minerals and transform what comes out of the tap into the type of water needed to make its beers. That leaves yeast, grain and hops. Most of the theories of how beer is brewed, as well as how various styles of beer can be created, involve one of these three elements.

For instance, there are two basic kinds of beer: lagers and ales. A main difference between them is the type of yeast used in the beer-making process. Ales use yeast that sits on top of the fermentation tank and is logically called a top-fermenting yeast. In addition, top-fermenters can be quick workers, meaning that an ale can ready to drink as early as ten days after the first steps of the beer-making process were started. Baltimore's first brewers, John Leonard and Elias Daniel Barnitz, made ales, as did the colonial brewers who followed in the subsequent decades. Ales happened to be preferred by the British, who ruled Maryland in the early 1700s.

Moreover, ales could be made at room temperatures and did not require vast storage space. Two hundred years later, these same factors—quick turnaround time, normal temperature requirements and easy storage—made this type of brewing attractive to a new generation of beer makers. The British Brewing Company in Glen Burnie, the state's first microbrewer, made ales, and when Sisson's brewpub in south Baltimore launched Maryland into the craft brewing

Introduction

revival, one its first beers was Stockade, an ale named in honor of the time when the town was surrounded by a stockade fence.

By contrast, a lager is made with yeast that sinks. It is a bottom-fermenter. A lager yeast takes its time, sometimes up to six weeks, to get the job done. It also likes to work in the cold, so when a brewer makes a lager, he puts it either in icy caves or in refrigerated lagering tanks and waits several weeks before bottling. Until the mid-1800s, most of the beers made were ales. Lagers did not take hold in Baltimore until the late 1800s, when George Bauernschmidt's Greenwood Brewery and John von der Horst's Eagle Brewery put in a mechanical refrigeration systems and made lagering less labor-intensive. A long line of Baltimore lagers followed, including National Premium, which in the 1940s was sold nationwide but only to selected, tony establishments such as the Plaza Hotel in New York. When Jerry Hoffberger got married in the mid-1940s, he and his bride, Alice, flew to Los Angeles, where at a party given in their honor by entertainer Victor Borge, National Premium was served. The popular but less expensive beer, National Bohemian, or "Natty Boh," is also a lager.

Today, the popular beers sold by Anheuser-Busch, In-Bev, Miller and Coors are light lagers, while area craft brewers like Clipper City Brewing in Halethorpe, Flying Dog Brewery in Frederick and some other brewpubs produce more full-bodied versions of a lager.

Brewers use a lot of grain when they make beer. Proof of grain's weighty impact can be seen by looking at the massive silos near big breweries or by asking any small brewer who has had to lug heavy tubs of spent grain out of the brew house. The majority of the grain that goes into beer is malted barley, also called malt. Both ales and lagers use it. Additionally, some brewers put rice in their recipes. When making a wheat beer, brewers add some wheat to the malt mixture. Corn is also sometimes used.

Malt matters. How much a brewer puts in his recipe, as well as what kind of malt he uses, affects the alcohol, the body and often the color of the beer. Malted barley comes in a variety of types (two-row or six-row) and a range of shades (pale, amber, crystal, chocolate and black). The shade of the malt depends on how it has been roasted in a kiln.

Careful brewers, like good chemists, keep close track of the amount of ingredients they put in their brews. One glimpse of how much "stuff" has been put in a beer is a measure called "specific gravity." Technically, specific gravity is measure of the weight of a beery liquid compared to water. But generally speaking, the more grain a brewer puts in his beer, the more its

Introduction

gravity and its cost of production increases. The Doppelbock, for instance, once made by the former Baltimore Brewing Company—a brew that has garnered a first place in the 1990s at the Great American Beer Festival in Colorado—used about twice the amount of malt in the recipe than goes into one of its standard-issue lagers. Resurrection, a big beer brewed by the Brewer's Art in Baltimore, has a specific gravity of 1.075, meaning that when it starts fermenting, this beer is 1.075 times denser than water.

Hops are also major players in the taste and the cost of a beer. Hops are like spices, small but potent components of the recipe that the brewer adds to the mix of grains and yeast to produce distinctive flavors and aromas. Hops get much of the credit for creating the bitter notes of a fine beer.

Traditionally, certain hops are added at certain points in the brewing process, such as when liquid called wort comes to a boil. But a fair amount of the brewer's art goes into deciding what kind of hops to use and when to use them. Brewers, like chefs, don't like to be held to one way of practicing their craft and have been known to get creative with the hops. Nonetheless, there are certain classic pairings. Take Pilsner, a type of lager originally modeled after the beer made in Pilsen but now brewed around the world. A hop commonly used in making Pilsner is Saaz. For English ales, the classic hop is Goldings.

Additionally, breweries choose between using the hop cone (the female flower of the hop plant) or pellets (plugs made from ground-up cones). In a tug of war common to many businesses, the brewer often lobbies to use the more expensive hops to give his brew a distinctive flavor, while the bookkeeper wants to know how the extra hop expense will make the bottom line look better. Hops also have an antiseptic feature, which is part of what made them popular in the days before refrigeration. If you hopped a beer, it lasted longer.

Having laid out these broad guidelines, there are, of course, myriad exceptions. There are beers that are made using a combination of ale and lager styles. There is the so-called California-common style of brewing, made popular by Anchor Brewing Company of San Francisco, which produces a bottom-fermented lager yeast working in warm, ale-like, temperatures.

Malt liquors, like National Brewing Company's Colt 45, delivered higher alcoholic punch, about 7 percent alcohol per volume compared to the normal 4–5 percent for beer, without upping the costly ingredients. Instead, it added sugar to its regular lager recipe. Some brewers use rye, oats, beet sugar, sorghum or even millet to make beer. But the appeal of these brews is not widespread.

Introduction

Light beers work on another side of the brewing equation. By using hungry yeasts that attack a brew's normally unfermentable complex sugars, and by artfully adding water to their recipes, modern brewers have produced a popular series of low-calorie, low-alcohol beers that promise to deliver "less" than their traditional brews—a promise that is widely kept.

Then there are the Belgian-style beers. The Belgian brewers seem to break all the conventions and have been successfully doing it for centuries. Their brown ales, for instance, can take months to mature, much longer than the supposed slow-maturing lagers. Their red ales are aged in wooden kegs, like wines. While brewers around the world try to keep their brewery hatches batted down and their yeasts under tight control, Belgians brewers in the Zenne River Valley have been known to take the tops off their vessels and invite Mother Nature to let the wild yeasts in and induce spontaneous fermentation to make a wheat beer. A beer made this way in this region is called a lambic beer. Sometimes fruits, like cherries and raspberries, are added to these spontaneously fermented beers.

Belgians also make witbier, or white beer, by using a mixture of wheat and tossed-in orange peel and coriander. So, in addition to traditional ingredients, the Belgians use air, fruit and herbs to make beer. Baltimore's modern Belgian-style brewers have adapted some of the old country ways. The Brewer's Art, a brewpub on North Charles, periodically makes a Belgian Brown ale with sour cherries called Charm City Sour Cherry. But it has never gone lambic, taking the tops off the tanks and letting the Baltimore air go to work on the beer. Common sense, not to mention the health department, rules against it.

Delving into a city's past teaches you things about the community you call home. I was impressed by the strong influence German culture had on Baltimore. Until World War I, notes from the city council meetings were printed in German as well as English. In the early 1900s, massive competitions of German choral music groups called Saengerfests were held in Baltimore's new Fifth Regiment Armory, with Baltimore brewers, especially Gunther's, telling the five thousand visiting singers that its beer was the *real* German brew. The old German picnic ground near Gay Street and another in Carroll Park are gone, but the city's newer brewers and tavern owners are reviving the beer garden concept. At one time there seemed to be several royal brewing families who attended the same church (Zion Lutheran), intermarried and seemed to name most of their sons John. A glance at the cooking recipes put out by the breweries in the 1950s and '60s (Globe, National and Gunther)

Introduction

found much Teutonic fare, such as a mixture of beer, egg yolks, lemon and cream called German Beer Soup.

I was also struck by the size and scope of the city's former breweries. These were big operations, employing hundreds. The George Bauernschmidt brewery on Gay Street turned out so much beer, more than 50,000 barrels in the early 1900s, that some of it was shipped back to Germany. His son, Frederick, is said to have produced 400,000 barrels per year. At its peak in the 1960s and 1970s, the Carling National operations in the Baltimore metro area produced more than 1 million barrels per year and employed almost one thousand workers. When you stand on the balconies atop the magnificent American Brewery building on Gay Street or the renovated National Brewing Company building on Conkling Street—a treat tour groups are offered during Baltimore Beer Week in October—the sweeping views of the city and the grandeur that was once industrial Baltimore are overwhelming.

Finally, the civic involvement and charitable giving of the city's brewers impressed me. There were many examples sprinkled through the years. In the 1920s, Frederick Bauernschmidt was a philanthropist who donated some $3 million to about thirty different groups, chief among them Union Memorial Hospital. He was keenly interested in helping members of the middle class pay their hospital bills and set up a fund to pay for such expenses. In addition, he put most of the family's real estate holdings in a trust that would generate funds to operate the Hospital for Consumptives at Eudowood and the Home for Incurables.

In Canton, John Frederick Wiessner, the owner of a brewery on the site of the old Fort Marshall, was the chief of the volunteer fire company. Upon his death in 1904, his home at Eastern and Highland Avenues was, as requested in his will, turned into a home for orphans.

Some of the contributions were personal. Frank B. Cahn, for instance, the head of Monumental Brewing Company, was a violinist who performed in local chamber music events. In 1953, he set up a fund at Baltimore Museum Art to endow an annual chamber music concert named in honor of his wife. And when the Baltimore Symphony Orchestra was raising money to stay in operation in 1943, among the female fundraisers was Mrs. Arthur Deute, wife of the president of National Brewing Company.

The roles played by the city brewing barons of the 1950s to secure professional football and baseball franchises for Baltimore have been well documented. There was some self-interest involved, as beer and sporting events are happy companions. But the largesse of the Hoffberger and

Introduction

Krieger families, once owners of National and Gunther breweries, is still felt in the city today in the foundations and institutions that their legacies support. *Town and Country* magazine estimated in 1983 that Jerry Hoffberger had donated more than $10 million to charities. The Krieger name, a testimony to the family's generosity, can be found on hospital and classroom buildings throughout the Baltimore metropolitan area.

In ways big and small, many of the city's brewers have made Baltimore, this sudsy city, a better place to live.

Early Brewing in Baltimore

Amid the Mud and the Wolves a Town and Its Breweries Are Born

Baltimore's proud brewing heritage began long before it had paved streets. Beer bubbled through its veins, but in its early days, Baltimore Town was far from the land of pleasant living. A visitor entered the town through one of three gates in a stockade fence erected to protect residents from predators. The lanes were muddy, and a traveler was likely to encounter a flock of hissing geese or herds of squealing hogs. Creatures from the nearby Jones Falls were nuisances, and tobacco was paid to citizens to keep the critters at bay. Fail to deliver three squirrel scalps or crow's heads to the justice of the peace every year, and you were fined two pounds of tobacco. On the other side of the ledger, if you produced a wolf's head, you got a tax credit of two hundred pounds of tobacco, a precursor to the city's current practice offering developers payments in lieu of taxes. A city shining on the hill it was not. Even its first brewer, John Leonard Barnitz, preferred to spend time on his farm in York County, Pennsylvania, rather than in town.

THE EARLY YEARS

Although Baltimore would emerge as the state's commercial hub, one brewer elsewhere in Maryland got the first hop, so to speak, on brewing. In 1703, Benjamin Fordham, a Londoner by birth who had tried his hand at brewing in Philadelphia before moving to Annapolis, made "table beer," a strongly hopped ale that appealed to the sailors, British and American, who frequented the then tiny, forty-home village of Annapolis. As Annapolis

Four derby-clad turn-of-the-century gentlemen enjoying their beer. *Courtesy CityLit.*

grew, so did Fordham's prominence. He became a city alderman and, along with the mayor, successfully petitioned the royal governor in 1708 to raise the status of Annapolis from a village to a city. He also established Maryland's maiden brewery in Annapolis. Forty-five years later, Barnitz and his son, Elias Daniel, opened Baltimore's pioneer brew house on Hanover Street about fifty feet south of Baltimore Street.

Success was far from certain, as Baltimore Town consisted of some sixty lots, not all of them occupied. Fires from flaming chimneys were a constant problem, and every homeowner was required to own a ladder capable of reaching his roof and battling the flames. During a bitter winter, portions of the town's stockade fence were pulled down and used as firewood. A mud hole on Market Street almost swallowed a drummer boy and his horse. A year later, in 1782, the streets were paved.

This type of city living held limited appeal for Barnitz, a native of Falkenstien, Germany, where he had learned the brewing craft. He established a brewery in Baltimore and, before that, one in York, Pennsylvania, and he was a founding member of Baltimore's Zion Lutheran Church, yet he did not reside in these towns. Instead, he retreated to his farm in Heidelberg Township in York County. He died a year after opening the Baltimore brewery and was buried in York County. His son took over the business. Barnitz's Brewery, which after a string of ten owners eventually became the city's noted Globe Brewery, rose from where the main entrance to the former Morris Mechanic Theater sits today.

A Satisfying History of Charm City Brewing

However, Baltimore beer makers soon made up for lost time. By 1784, the city boasted not only the largest brewery in the state but also the largest in the nation: the Thomas Peters and Company. Later known as Baltimore Strong Beer Brewery, the Peters brewery sat at East Lombard and the Jones Falls, near "Brewer's Park." Now home to a Marriott hotel, this site housed nine brewing operations over a stretch of ninety-three years. Thomas Peters partnered with his father-in-law, Dr. Edward Johnson, and their ale quickly pleased the populace. A few short years later, Johnson was elected mayor of Baltimore, in which position he served from 1808 to 1824. Johnson found the demands of simultaneously brewing and governing too heavy a load and eventually sold the brew house at auction in 1813 to George I. Brown, who in turn sold it to Eli Claggett in 1818.

Brown, a merchant who lived in the neighborhood, owned the brewery for only five years. But in those five years, he used it to make a significant mark on history. It was on the floor of this newly purchased brewery that seamstress Mary Pickersgill sewed the massive American flag that would later inspire Francis Scott Key to write "The Star-Spangled Banner."

Earlier that year, Joshua Barney, commodore of the Chesapeake Bay Flotilla, asked Pickersgill to sew a giant American flag for Fort McHenry. The thirty- by forty-two-foot flag measured too large to fit in her modest eighteen-foot-wide home (now the historic site of the Star-Spangled Banner Flag House). So when Pickersgill needed to stretch out the flag and evenly space the stars, she went around the corner to the local brewery. There she was allowed to use a section of the malt house to unfurl and assemble the flag. While today, flag etiquette demands that it be burned if it touches the ground, no such feeling existed in 1813. Pickersgill's daughter, Caroline T. Purdy, recalled seeing her mother at the malt house "down on the floor, placing the stars."

The floor was probably wood, and since the structure had recently been rebuilt after a fire in 1812, it was in relatively good shape. When the brewery was auctioned in 1813, an advertisement pitching its features to buyers described "two malt houses, 100 feet long by 30 feet, with [a] granary over each." It went on, in the flowery prose of realtors, to describe the brewery and its buildings as "the most complete establishment of the kind in the United States."

A painting by artist R. McGill Mackall hangs in Baltimore's Flag House Museum and shows the seamstress hard at work next to barrels of Claggett beer. But records show that in 1813 the brewery was owned by Brown. While the ownership of the building might be debated, historians nonetheless agree that the "Stars and Stripes" that flew over Fort McHenry was sewn on the floors of a Baltimore brewery.

The city's population grew from 80,000 in 1830 to 225,000 in 1863, and so did the number of its breweries. From 1833 to 1850, for instance, the number of beer makers jumped from just four to twenty-nine. Many of these new breweries were perched alongside the Jones Falls, a location that in those ecologically insensitive times afforded easy dumping of brewery waste into the stream. Although Native Americans once bathed in the Jones Falls, at a spot later known as Bath Street, the stream was far from pristine. Frogs and mosquitoes thrived at a marshy bend in the stream called Steiger's Meadow, near what is now the Jones Falls and Franklin Street. Frequent floods, including a big one in 1837, wiped out or damaged Jones Falls breweries, including one at Holliday and Hillen Streets owned by Marcus McCausland. This enterprising Irishman ran many ventures in Baltimore and presided over the "Office of the Scavenger," which meant that he landed the contract to clean the streets. Some of McCausland's brewery workers

An early view of a bridge across the Jones Falls, a stream that regularly flooded and a place many early brewers dumped their industrial waste. The Shot Tower is in the background. *Courtesy CityLit.*

lived in "Limerick," a lowland north of city hall and west of the Jones Falls, near the city jail. The neighborhood was home to pickpockets and thugs. Strangers were warned not to venture there after dark.

Other noted breweries that set up business in different parts of town were the Jacob Seeger Brewery, built in 1854 at Pratt Street and Frederick Avenue, and the Mount Royal Brewery, established by John George Hoffman in 1860 at the corner of Twenty-third Street and Huntingdon Avenue, near a group of row houses known as "Good Husbands Row," said to be occupied by loafing, beer-drinking spouses.

Irish moss was used by brewers at the time to clarify their beers, cream of tartar was thought to soften the water used in brewing and dissolve impurities and gum improved a beer's head. The spent grain or malt extract leftover from the brewing process was fed to children.

Captain John Daniel Danels, who lived from 1783 until 1855 and whose Baltimore-based fleet would regularly attack British privateers, described the types of beer made by early Baltimore brewers. They included, he said, ale (a heavier form of beer than in general use), stout (a strong dark beer), porter (a weak stout), strong beer (a brew that had strong taste not high alcohol), small beer (a low alcohol brew), table beer (stronger and made of better ingredients than small beer) and ship's beer (a brew that often spoiled).

The Germans Arrive

One reason for the increase in the city's brewing activity involved a wave of immigrants from Germany. Historians generally cite two main reasons why Germans left their homeland in the mid-nineteenth century and arrived on the banks of the Patapsco River. First, Germans came to the United States to escape a series of wars and compulsory military service. Second, Baltimore was the American port at which the North German Lloyd Steamship Company dropped anchor. The ships unloaded at Locust Point, and many German passengers went no farther, making Baltimore their new home.

In the years before prohibition, the Baltimore brewing scene was dominated by a thicket of German families. Starting with the city's first brewer, Barnitz, and continuing through the sudsy reigns of the Bauernschmidts, the Wiessners and the Brehms, many of the city's brewers worshiped at the same church, Zion Lutheran. Sitting on Holliday Street and located just east of Baltimore City Hall, the handsome brick church still has vestiges

Baptismal font in Zion Lutheran Church donated by Frank Steil, a nineteenth-century brewer, one of many who belonged to the church. *Photo by Alexander D. Mitchell IV.*

of its connection to former brewers and the brewers' largesse. The marble baptismal font was a gift in 1905 from Frank Steil, an early brewer. A stained-glass window showing St. John the Evangelist was given in 1897 in memory of another brewer, John F. Wiessner, and his wife, Sarah, and a wooden pew still carries the nameplate "Bauernschmidt," marking where members of the brewing family once sat during services.

One member of the Zion congregation, Mark Duerr, has delved into the history of the church and its brewers. His work, printed here in the appendix, provides clear evidence of the strong ties between the church and the city's German brewers. Moreover, his capsule descriptions of the members of the prominent brewing families—some sharing not only the same surname but also the same first name—serve as excellent guideposts in navigating the city's early brewing history.

A Satisfying History of Charm City Brewing

One young German arrival in Baltimore was not content to stay put. He ventured farther inland to eventually make American brewing history. David Gottlieb Yuengling, the twenty-two-year-old son of a Württemberg butcher, debarked in Baltimore in 1828 but, one year later, moved to Pottsville, Pennsylvania, laying the foundations for Yuengling Brewing, the oldest brewery in the United States. Dick Yuengling said that topography drove his great-great-grandfather to leave Baltimore for the mountains of Pennsylvania. Yuengling wanted to build his brewery on a mountain with dark, cool caves where beer could properly age. Baltimore must have looked pretty flat to this German immigrant to force him north until he found the perfect mountain.

But many other German immigrants and expert brewers found Baltimore ideal for beer making, so much so that two areas in the city developed reputations as brewery neighborhoods: Brewers Row and Brewers Hill.

Until 1860, most of Baltimore's beer makers produced only enough beer to quench the thirst of customers who frequented their taverns (brewpubs in today's parlance) on a regular basis. But the buildings constructed along Brewers Row were bigger and aimed to please a larger audience (predecessors, in a way, of craft breweries). George Rost, a native of Bavaria, set the tone of brewing in the neighborhood.

From 1863 to 1920, the J.F. Wiessner brewery on Gay Street was one of the largest on Brewers Row. *Drawing courtesy CitLit.*

Painting of Standard Brewery, Gay Street and Patterson Park Avenue, successor to brewery started in 1854 by George Rost, the godfather of early Baltimore brewers. *Courtesy David Donovan Collection. Photo by Edward Brown.*

William Kelley—who in 1965 published a definitive chronicle of beer making in the Free State, *Brewing in Maryland*—characterized Rost as the "father of Baltimore brewmasters." Rost set up Rost's Brewery in 1851 in an expanse running between Gay Street and the 2200 block of North Avenue. Instead of cooling his beer in mountain caves like Yuengling, Rost dug tunnels under Baltimore where he stored barrels of his freshly brewed lager to ferment (one meaning of the German word *lager* being "store"). He also erected a beer garden next to the brewery called George Rost's Meadow, in the then leafy climes of North Avenue. There Baltimoreans drank German-style beer and sang German drinking songs such as "Bierwalzer," a song with easy lyrics—"La, la, la"—that only require participants to stomp their feet and clink their steins.

In 1866, Baltimore's target range, a Schuetzen Verein, or a private park and picnic grounds for German families, was established within earshot of the brewery on Gay Street. There marksmen could fire a few rounds and then repair to nearby breweries for refreshments.

A Satisfying History of Charm City Brewing

As Laura Rice observed in her 2002 book *Maryland History in Prints*, published by the Maryland Historical Society, the park was just a few blocks away from plants run by Wiessner, Rost and Bauernschmidt. These breweries, Rice wrote, both provided liquid solace for the park patrons and also featured their own beer gardens.

The annual Schuetzenfest was a major event on the city's social calendar, attended by mayors and throngs numbering five thousand. It resembled a modern-day beer festival, with one noteworthy exception: men shooting rifles. A marksman who emerged at the top of the fest's annual shooting match was crowned "king" of the fest. A "queen" was picked by the president of the Schuetzen Society and was adorned with a heavy gold locket that marked her royal status. Bands played, dancers whirled and the scene, according to newspaper reports, was "busy, animated and ever-changing." Quite a party. This site was known as the Eastern Schuetzen. The Western Schuetzen, a popular recreation spot for German speakers in the two decades after the Civil War, was located in what is now Carroll Park.

One of the workers at the Rost brewery, John Wiessner, thought that there existed an opportunity for another brewery in this suds-loving town. He

In the mid-nineteenth century, Baltimore benefited from a wave of German immigrants who brought their large families and love of beer with them from the homeland. *Courtesy CityLit.*

ventured out on his own and started John Wiessner and Sons in 1863 in the 1700 block of Gay Street. Things went so well for Wiessner that in 1887 he built an even larger brewery, the five-story Bavarian Gothic brew house later known as the American Brewery. To this day, the massive building looms over east Baltimore.

Also following Rost to Brewers Row was George Bauernschmidt, one of three beer-brewing brothers from Bavaria. In 1864, Bauernschmidt ended a brewing operation on 323 West Pratt Street that he had run with his brother, John J. Jr., and moved to a more spacious and modern building in the 1500 block of Gay Street. Bauernschmidt's new operation, called Greenwood Brewery, would take two progressive steps. First, he bottled his own beer rather than farming out the task to bottling companies. Second, instead of using ice hauled down from Maine to chill his beer, he installed a mechanical refrigeration system. The early refrigeration systems, like early automobiles, were prone to breakdowns. Ammonia leaked out of the pipes of an early refrigeration compressor at Greenwood, ruining an entire batch of beer. This foul-up presented a sales opportunity that was pounced on by a nearby rival, the J.F. Wiessner Brewing Company, whose beers were still cooled by ice.

Ice had its loyalists, among them beer drinkers and tavern keepers, who preferred their brews cooled by "Maine ice," massive hunks of frozen water that were regularly delivered to Baltimore from Kennebec by a fleet of five-masted schooners. However, cellarmen who had to work in the damp climes created by melting ice—a cause, they said, of pneumonia, tuberculosis and aching joints—welcomed refrigeration. Many were delighted to shed their rubber boots and the heavy work of hauling ice. Eventually, refrigeration systems improved, and this enabled brewers to increase production, store beer longer and get rid of the old-fashioned beer cellars, not to mention avoid the headaches associated with handling melting ice.

The task of putting beer in a bottle—tricky even by today's standards—was more burdensome for early brewers. Not only was bottling expensive, but storing the bottles also took up valuable space in the brewery. Then there was the problem of leaky lids. But in 1892, William Painter, a Baltimore machinist, devised and patented the crown cork closure method that ensured tight-fitting lids and a better bottled beer. Painter's work led to the formation of Baltimore's Crown Cork & Seal Company, and his method of sealing a bottle was adopted by breweries around the world.

In 1900, the Bauernschmidt brewery boom continued when George's son, Frederick, built an even larger brew house at Hillen and Monument Streets.

A Satisfying History of Charm City Brewing

The summer home of Frederick Bauernschmidt and his wife, Agnes, this magnificent structure was built in about 1906 in Middle River on land that was once owned by Enoch Pratt. *Courtesy CityLit.*

The growing business contributed to the Bauernschmidts' economic impact on the city and their influence on city life in general. Baltimore's prominent and affluent citizens visited their opulent family summer home on Bauernschmidt Road in Essex, which with its wraparound porches and huge cupola offered spectacular views of Middle River and the Chesapeake Bay. Built on land that was once owned by philanthropist Enoch Pratt, it remains an architectural marvel. The family's city home, at North and Broadway, is also a landmark, designed by George A. Frederick, the architect who built Baltimore City Hall (it is slated to become offices for an expanded Blacks in Wax Museum).

Marie Bauernschmidt, a south Baltimore girl who married William, Frederick Bauernschmidt's brother, regularly used her election eve radio show *Mrs. B. Speaks Her Mind* to lambaste local politicians in 1940s. "Cutting politicians down to size," wrote local historian Gilbert Sandler in a 1991 *Sun* column, "became not just her style but her passion." She even went after what she considered the inappropriate use of beer. An article in the *Sun* on May 2, 1937, noted that Mrs. Bauernschmidt was "horrified to discover that some Locust Point mothers were feeding their babies beer and pickles." She died in 1962.

Another major brewer to occupy Brewers Row was John von der Horst, who combined an interest in beer with his family's passion for baseball. In 1866, he teamed up with brewmaster Andreas Ruprechet and moved into a former oilcloth factory on Gay Street near North Avenue to set up Eagle Brewery and Malt House. A little short of twenty years later, his son, Harry R. von der Horst, widely known as Henry, moved his baseball team, the Orioles, to a field he built at Twenty-fifth Street and Greenmount Avenue. After his father died in 1894, Henry tried to introduce Baltimore to its first light beer, Cabinet, which used rice and lightly roasted malt and was pale. Most beers of that time were heavy brews made with dark malt. This was pale in color and low in alcohol and was aimed at consumers with discriminating tastes—cabinet members. Not surprisingly, it flopped.

Today, such a mixture of baseball and beer might be called "synergy"; back then, it was simply business as usual. The Orioles played in the American Association, a circuit dubbed "the beer and whiskey league" because so many of its teams were owned by brewers and distillers.

Meanwhile, on the east side of Baltimore near Conkling and O'Donnell Streets, the second brewery neighborhood was taking shape. Brewers Hill was another epicenter of brewing in the city, and it served as home to thirty-seven breweries over the years. Within this climate of increased competition, some of the newer brewers encountered trouble paying the bills. Many of these breweries were ripe for takeovers. One such enterprise ready to snatch up these struggling companies was that of the Straus brothers, Henry and Levy, who along with Alexander Bell ran a malt operation, H. Straus Brothers & Bell. The Straus business gave the beginning brewers malt on credit, and when the brewer failed to pay the bills, it assumed control. The Straus operation was able to acquire the Rost Brewery this way.

In 1885, the two younger Straus family members, Joseph J. and William L., two of the seven sons of malt baron Levy Straus, took over a bankrupt east Baltimore operation run by Anna and Frederick Wunder and christened it the National Brewing Company. National became one of the city's landmark breweries, eventually brewing two beers that would dominate the Chesapeake Bay region: National Premium and National Bohemian.

A Satisfying History of Charm City Brewing

THE BEER TRUSTS

The malt makers' practice of picking up troubled breweries one at a time was soon overwhelmed by two beer trusts that took over Baltimore breweries en masse. These takeovers led to the biggest beer fights in Baltimore's pre-prohibition history, the formation and ultimate failure of two "beer trusts." The initial trust, called the Maryland Brewing Company, or MBC ran from March 1899 to August 1901 and consolidated seventeen breweries into one behemoth. Those seventeen were George Bauernschmidt Brewing Company, George Gunther Brewing Company, the Globe brewery (known

When brewer John Bauernschmidt died in 1879, his wife, Elizabeth, brought her brother, John Marr, into the business. The west Baltimore operation became known as the Spring Garden Brewery of the Bauernschmidt and Marr Brewing Company, was sold in 1899 to a British syndicate and was later swallowed by two beer trusts. *Courtesy David Donovan Collection. Photo by Edward Brown.*

Painting of Wehr-Hobelmann-Gottlieb, an 1881 malt house and brewery that later became Globe Brewing Company. *Courtesy David Donovan Collection. Photo by Edward Brown.*

then as Wehr-Hobelman-Gottleib Brewing and Malting Company), National Brewing Company, Eigenbrot Brewing Company, Bay View Brewery, George Brehm Brewery, Germania Brewing Company, Oriental Brewing Company, John F. Wiessner & Brother Brewing Company, Baltimore Brewing Company, John B. Berger Brewing Company, Sebastian Helldorfer Sons Brewing Company, J.H. von der Horst and Son Brewing Company and three breweries—Darley Park, Bauernschmidt and Marr and Mount—that, ten years earlier, had formed an alliance with a British syndicate and called themselves Baltimore United Breweries Limited. It was merger mania, but it didn't work.

When the first trust, Maryland Brewing Company, faltered, the second—Gottleib-Bauernschmidt-Straus Brewing Company, or GBS—took over. It consolidated the remaining breweries and ran from 1901 until 1920.

In modern terms, these trusts were similar to mergers. The officers of the trusts were drawn from the ranks of the absorbed breweries. The theory was that efficiencies from the large-scale operation would drive down costs and make brewing beer profitable for all members of the trust. Indeed, Richard

A Satisfying History of Charm City Brewing

Sperry, the first president of Maryland Brewing Company, boldly predicted that all of the city's breweries, not just the initial seventeen that signed on, would eventually fall under the control of the MBC.

It did not work out that way. The MBC failed to generate anything close to its ballyhooed profits. Some breweries that were initially sold to the trust were bought back a few years later by their original owners at much reduced prices. Two prime examples were John F. Wiessner's brewery in east Baltimore, called Fort Marshall, as it resided on the site of a former Civil War fort, and George Brehm's brewery near what is now Brehm's Lane and Erdman Avenue. They made money when they sold to the trust and then were able to regain their breweries at bargain prices. Another brewer, George Gunther Sr., outsmarted the trusts in a different way. The senior Gunther sold his brewery to the MBC trust, but his son, George Jr., opened a new brewery right across the street. The trust sued, claiming that this violated an anti-competition clause, but the lawsuit failed. Eventually, the Gunther family bought its original brewery back.

The trusts had labor troubles. Shortly after the MBC was formed, its brewery workers went on strike until the trust guaranteed them a uniform working day of nine hours in the winter and ten in the summer. Many were shifted to work at different breweries, sometimes with a resulting loss of wages. Then there were hurt feelings. As beer historian Art Distelrath Jr. chronicled in "Merger Mania" in the January–February 2006 issue of the *American Breweriana* journal, the brewers and saloonkeepers with ties to the closed plants were none too happy with being told that their operations were obsolete. "These smaller breweries had strong neighborhood ties and the locals perceived the MBC claim that they antiquated and obsolete as dishonest and greedy," Distelrath wrote.

One set of brewing brothers, Charles and George Schlaffer, were so miffed that their Oriental Brewery was closed and that they were not given lofty positions within the MBC that they struck a temporary deal with a brewer in Washington, D.C., Christian Heurich. The Baltimore brothers promised to deliver to Heurich all Baltimore drinkers who were upset that their neighborhood breweries had closed. The principals at MBC quickly welcomed the Schlaffers back into the fold.

Meanwhile, independent breweries that had not joined the trust continued to give the trust stiff competition. As was true of the city during the Civil War, there were family members on both sides of the battle. Two of the city's prominent brewing families, the Bauernschmidts and the Wiessners, had some men who joined the trusts and some who remained independent brewers. There were ongoing price wars starting in 1899, when the MBC temporarily lowered the price of a barrel of beer to $4.50 from the usual $5.00 range. Later, the pendulum swung in the other direction, and independent brewers were able to sell their beer at $0.50 to $1.00 less than the $6.00 per barrel the trust charged.

The independent brewers, chief among them Fred Bauernschmidt, prevailed in the early going. After a year or two, prominent members of the MBC trust began to pull away. One of the dissenters was George Brehm. By May 1910, a court had declared MBC insolvent, and a few months later, a new corporation, Gottleib-Bauernschmidt-Straus, succeeded it. GBS closed still more breweries, among them Helldorfer, Germania and Von der Horst, but the second trust was more brand-savvy than its predecessor.

Advertisements touted the sparkling Adonis beer made by the trust's Eigenbrot brewery in west Baltimore, its Globe brewery turned out a brew called Munich and Darley Park, a brewery that took its name from a park off Harford Road, made a brew called Ideal. GBS tried all manner of tactics to appease its main competitor, Fred Bauernschmidt, whose beer was less expensive than that produced by the trust. The trust even named Bauernschmidt's brother-in-law, Globe's Albert Wehr, as its president in hopes of making peace. But the rivalry continued. By 1915, GBS had just three plants: Eigenbrot, National and Globe. It continued operating until it was met with even stiffer competition, something called prohibition. Of the GBS breweries, only Globe operated during the Prohibition era. It produced a near beer and, once the ban was lifted, a brew called Arrow.

In assessing why the trusts failed, Distelrath ticked off a host of reasons: "Too many plants purchased at high prices, poor management decisions and relations with workers, and competition from large, well-organized independents."

Local pride also played a role. It was a factor cited by William Kelley, author of the definitive *Brewing in Maryland*, in his summation of why the trusts failed. "When the old established breweries lost their well-known and often well-liked ownerships, and passed into impersonal hands," Kelley wrote, "many consumers switched to a brewery where traditional conditions and independence prevailed."

Bigger did not turn out to be better for most of the Baltimore breweries associated with the beer trusts. But for all the fervor of the battles between the trusts and the independents, combatants agreed that drinking beer was an established part of American life. That belief was challenged, sometimes with an axe, by the supporters of prohibition.

A Satisfying History of Charm City Brewing

Prohibition: "A Horror"

In the 1920s, prohibition was the law of the land. Beer taps dried up, and breweries scrambled to stay alive. *Evening Sun* scribe H.L. Mencken railed against Carrie Nation and her temperance troops, calling prohibition "a horror." Mencken, like many thirsty residents of Baltimore, took to brewing his own beer in his Union Square home. He usually brewed on Sunday and bottled on Wednesday. He had a secret ingredient, milk of magnesia—which, modern brewers explain, contains magnesium, which the yeast in the beer needs to thrive. Even so, many of his beers became "bombs."

"Last night I had three quart bottles in my side yard, cooling in a bucket," he wrote in a letter to his friend Harry Richel. "Two went off at once, bringing my neighbor out of his house with yells. He thought that Soviets had seized the town." As Daniel Okrent pointed out in his 2010 book *Last Call*, many residents of Baltimore did their best to pretend that the ban on alcohol did not apply to them. Speakeasy operators who regularly contributed to a fund for "disabled policemen" were excused from court appearances. When Maryland legislators refused to pass a state law enforcing prohibition, it was dubbed the "Free State" by *Baltimore Sun* editor Hamilton Owens, a moniker it still carries.

Describing the "wet" environment of the town, H.L. Mencken wrote to F. Scott Fitzgerald, "Baltimore is knee-deep in excellent beer. I begin to believe in prayer." Nonetheless, prohibition was law, and breweries turned out nonalcohol brews in response. Of these so-called buzzless beers, Arrow Special was a local favorite brewed by Globe, which traced its lineage back to John Leonard Barnitz, the city's first brewer. Arrow Special promised quaffers that it would "hit the spot," a slogan that emerged from a citywide contest to stir up interest in this malty near beer containing less than 0.5 percent alcohol by volume. More importantly, the buzzless beer kept the brew house functioning. When prohibition was lifted in 1933, Globe was among the first breweries to quench the city's built-up thirst for "real beer."

Mencken, in a much-publicized photograph, bellied up to the bar at the Rennert Hotel and downed an Arrow, and according to newspaper accounts, "the champion of better beer was grinning and his blue Nordic eyes were dancing" as the so-called high priest of brew issued his verdict on his first post-prohibition beer: "Pretty good. Not bad at all."

Prohibition had a devastating effect on breweries. Plants that had been producing thousands of barrels of beer per year and employing hundreds

Thirsty Baltimore beer drinkers wait outside Gunther Brewery at end of prohibition. News-American *photo from Special Collections, University of Maryland Libraries, used with permission of Hearst Communications, Inc., Hearst Newspapers Division.*

of men were put out of business and the workers put on the street. A prime example of the destructive power of prohibition is the tale of Baltimore's Monumental Brewing Company.

Located at the corners of East Lombard, Eaton, Haven and Baltimore Streets in east Baltimore, a section of the city that was home to dozens of breweries, Monumental was a major operation. It had some trouble getting off the ground. It started off in 1898 as the Monarch Brewing Company, but a few years later, when construction on its grounds was still going on, the money ran out. A fresh supply of investors, many of them saloon owners, chipped in, and the plant was completed and the brewery renamed Monumental.

Monumental began brewing in September 1900. Towering some six stories, laid out for an annual production of 300,000 barrels, it was one of the first in the city to rely on refrigeration, rather than icy underground cellars, to store its beer. Its executives, Frank B. Cahn, a former lawyer turned investment banker, and Peter Schmidt, a baker, tapped the neighborhood

A Satisfying History of Charm City Brewing

talent pool, hiring brewer John Kessler, who had worked at a nearby brewery, Franz Schlaffer's Oriental Brewery at Conkling and Fait Streets. Another east Baltimore man, William L. Strauss, who had served at another neighborhood brewery, National, was brought in as president, succeeding Arnold E. Hillegeist.

For twenty years, the operation prospered. Brewing with water drawn from artesian wells on the property, Monumental's Perfect Brew brand sold well, especially since its sixteen-ounce bottle offered several more ounces of beer than the twelve- and fourteen-ounce bottles of its competitors. The brewery expanded, enlarging its stock house and building a new four-story bottling plant. Its influence reached into the South, and in 1912 it refurbished a large storage depot in Norfolk, Virginia.

But this successful run came to a halt with the arrival of prohibition. With the ratification of the Eighteenth Amendment prohibiting the manufacture, sale and transporting of intoxicating beverages, which the Volstead Act defined as any containing more than 0.5 percent of alcohol by volume, the brewery was in trouble. In 1920, Monumental began closing down, selling its sixty-five brewery-owned saloons at auction. The plant was sold to a meatpacker, Jones and Lamb Company, which a few years later sold it to another meatpacking firm, Shafer & Company. An attempt to revive the Monumental brewery after the return of legal beer in 1933 failed to arouse interest.

Once prohibition had ended, Baltimore's thirst for beer grew even stronger. Several breweries were poised to dominate, but the one that would rise to the top was none other than the National Brewing Company.

National Beer

Glory, Fading and Resurrection

During the 1950s and 1960s, two beers, National Bohemian and National Premium, were the toasts of the town. With its massive plant in east Baltimore staffed by hundreds of loyal locals, the National Brewing Company covered Baltimore like its dreaded summer humidity—it was everywhere.

Snap on the television, and there on Channel 2 was *The National Sports Parade*, an afternoon sports roundup hosted by young Jim McKay and sponsored by National Brewing Company. Tune in to the televised "wrasslin matches" to watch Gorgeous George or Strangler Lewis go at it in the Coliseum on Monroe Street near North Avenue, and emcee Bailey Goss would holler "Whoa-ho!" and remind the racially integrated crowd that the matches were sponsored by National Beer. For the bowlers, and Baltimore had alleys full of them, there was the *Duckpins for Dollars*, another TV show presided over by Goss and sponsored by National. While the broadcasters for the Orioles and Colts were hired by competing breweries—at one time, Colts announcers were told to describe a successful extra-point attempt as "Good as Gunther's"—National hired an impressive lineup, including Goss, Ernie Harwell and Chuck "Ain't the Beer Cold" Thompson to describe the games and fill the airways with mentions of the brewery's regal pilsner National Premium and its easy-to-drink companion, National Bohemian.

Topping it all off was National's "Land of Pleasant Living" advertising campaign, animated spots featuring singing clams, a warbling troubadour and a catchy theme song touting the beer brewed on the shores of the Chesapeake Bay.

A Satisfying History of Charm City Brewing

National Brewing Company, circa 1940. *Courtesy Baltimore Museum of Industry.*

"If you were in a bar in Baltimore during the 1950s," said John Steadman, a sports columnist for the *News-American* and the *Baltimore Sun* newspapers, "and somebody said 'Gimme a Bud,' you knew the guy was from out-of-town."

THE HOFFBERGERS

The Hoffbergers, a family with deep roots in Baltimore, owned National. From bull roasts to ballgames, virtually every gathering and event in the metropolitan area served National beer. In short, National was as proud and parochial as the Baltimore populace.

The Hoffbergers took over National just before prohibition ended in 1933. The brewery complex at O'Donnell and Conkling Streets was then known as Gottleib-Bauernschmidt-Straus, which emerged through the tangle of history from the brewery started there by Frederick and Anna Wunder. Already prominent in the Baltimore scene, the Hoffbergers ran coal, ice and oil businesses, as well as dairy, poultry and bakery operations. Trucks with the name "Hoffberger" emblazoned on the side rolled through town. Samuel H. Hoffberger, one of seven sons of Charles and Sarah Hoffberger, landed the job of running the brewery. By the end of World War II, when Samuel's son, Jerold (or Jerry), took over the operation in 1946, the brewery was poised to battle the Gunther, Globe, American and Free State breweries for the lion's share of the Baltimore beer market.

Young Jerry was a reluctant standard-bearer. Repeating a story told at Hoffberger family gatherings, David Hoffberger recalled that his father initially declined the brewery job, claiming that he did not know the beer business. But the family persisted, and Jerry agreed after stipulating that he—not his father or any other older family member—would be in charge. "He said, 'I have to be the president, not me working for you,'" son David Hoffberger recounted.

Hoffberger utilized the marketing skills of Arthur H. Deute, a former advertising executive with New York's Ruppert Brewery. He also tapped the production know-how of Carl R. Kreitler, a brewmaster with a penchant for quality. While Kreitler supervised the modernization and expansion of the

Carl Kreitler, the highly touted if somewhat dictatorial brewmaster at National Brewing Company from 1933 to 1946. *Courtesy Baltimore Museum of Industry.*

A Satisfying History of Charm City Brewing

east Baltimore plant, which by 1954 turned out 1 million barrels of beer per year, Deute worked on marketing angles, including using the one-eyed "Mr. Boh" character that became a fixture in televised beer commercials.

Later, Hoffberger added the talents of Dawson L. Farber Jr., who started as a forty-seven-dollars-per-week beer salesmen and rose to Hoffberger's number-one assistant.

During the two and half decades that Hoffberger owned both the Baltimore Orioles and National Brewing Company, he had a habit of shifting personnel between the brewery and other family enterprises. In 1965, Frank Cashen was heading up National's advertising department when Hoffberger sent him over to the Orioles to become general manager.

Cashen recalled that both at the brewery and at the ballpark Hoffberger's management style allowed his people free reign. "Jerry gave you a lot personal freedom," Cashen said. "Hoffberger forged close personal relationships with the men he worked with. I played tennis with Jerry every week at the courts at the College of Notre Dame. You don't normally do things like that with your boss."

National beer trucks lined up outside its east Baltimore plant. *Courtesy Baltimore Museum of Industry.*

Workers at the brewery, where many landed their jobs because they were the son or relative of someone already on the payroll, remarked on Hoffberger's personal touch.

"He was a pretty nice man to work for," John Matoska recalled in the film *Mr. Boh's Brewery*, a 2006 documentary made by Alex Castro that told the tale of the brewery through the voices of the men who had worked there. "You were some kid working in the brewery, and he [Hoffberger] would come through on weekends…and he knew your name," Matoksa said. Another longtime brewery employee, Joe "Reds" Harper, told in the film how "Mr. Hoffberger" lent him money to buy a car. Jerome DiPaolo, head of the sales force, said that when one of his children fell out of a tree and broke an arm, Hoffberger dispatched an ambulance. "He was very interested in the family," DiPaolo said.

National jousted with Gunther and other local breweries to ally itself with another fixture on the local sports landscape: the Baltimore Colts. National tied its logo to team pictures and sponsored *Corralin' the Colts*, a television program that featured Colt players recounting the team's latest game.

Workers loading cases of beer from National, the brewery that controlled more than 60 percent of the Baltimore market in the 1950s. *Courtesy David Hoffberger.*

A Satisfying History of Charm City Brewing

National had a crackerjack sales team headed by DiPaolo, a colorful and demanding leader who occasionally ended his pep talks to his troops by turning off the lights in a meeting room and tossing a lighted firecracker into the crowd. "Instant motivation," DiPaolo explained. He got results. "We had a well-run sales department," recalled Robert W. Kroeger, whose career at National ran from 1960 to 1975 and who, in the late 1960s, oversaw marketing efforts in fourteen states from Maine to North Carolina.

DiPaolo's salesmen worked night and day, Kroeger recalled during a 2011 telephone conversation from his home in Newburn, North Carolina. The National salesmen made about $18,000 per year, about half the take-home pay of the unionized beer truck drivers; however, Kroeger said, they outpaced the competition. "Gunther, Free State [and] American were not really threats," Kroeger said. "They did not have our sales team or advertising dollars."

On the neighborhood level, a National salesman knew that if a community supper, talent show or smoker—a gathering of men featuring sports films, cigars and beer—were held in his territory, he was expected to be there pouring the product. National also dispatched beer "drummers" to taverns to buy a round of National beer for the customers and thereby perhaps "drum up" some new business. At one point in the 1950s, the only two establishments in Baltimore that did not carry National beer were Alonso's and the Greenspring Inn, but eventually they were won over. Each of the 2,700 establishments in the Baltimore metropolitan area that had a beer license carried National beer, a market penetration that, according to DiPaolo, was unequaled by any brewery in the country.

The brewery operated its own fleet of trucks, offered the then rare perk of sending top salesmen and their families on exotic vacations and bought four hours of time on that strange new gadget called "television," filling the afternoon with variety shows hosted by Goss and Jim McManus (later known to world as ABC's Jim McKay).

Also fueling National's successful ride was an advertising campaign that was one of the first to rely on humor and regional pride to sell beer. It was the work of Brod Doner's agency, a Detroit outfit that, in return for getting the National beer account, agreed to set up a Baltimore office. The agency went on to become a leader in Baltimore's advertising community.

60 Percent of the Beer Market

The cumulative effect of good beer, aggressive salesmanship and creative advertising brewed success. National climbed to the top of the Baltimore market, and its management systems began to be noticed by the brewing industry. "We became a power in the beer industry," recalled Farber, Hoffberger's senior vice-president. "In 1954, we had sixty percent of the Baltimore beer business."

While the star of the show was National Bohemian, its ritzy brother, National Premium, also did well. National Premium's icon, Mr. Pilsner (originally spelled with an extra "e," Pilsener), sported a monocle and often donned a tuxedo.

First brewed in 1936, National Premium was the proud product of brewmaster Kreitler. Kreitler joined National shortly after repeal of prohibition and oversaw the remodeling of an old east Baltimore brewery that had been shuttered during the dry years of 1920–33. An exacting (some

National Brewing company employees and friends "harvesting" hops. *Courtesy David Hoffberger.*

would say dictatorial) brewer, Kreitler imported a yeast from the Carlsburg brewery in Demark, he grew hops on his 247-acre farm near Jarrettsville and was renowned in the brewing industry for his skills. National touted Kreitler's expertise, proclaiming in a 1941 advertisement in the *Baltimore Sun* that while there were more than five hundred beers in America, the "decisive element which distinguishes one beer from the others is the skill, the blending, the sure touch" of its master brewer. .

National Premium billed itself as the "coast-to-coast party beer, a few cents more but well worth it." It sold in the 1940s for fifteen cents per bottle compared to ten cents for a bottle of National Bohemian. It was well received locally. "It is smooth, mild, not bitter and it never gives me a headache," Nancy O'Connell wrote in 1937 as part of a campaign that asked Baltimore residents to write testimonials about the beer. National Premium also had a national and international following. It was served at the Plaza Hotel and Lindy's restaurant in New York, at the Ivanhoe restaurant in Chicago and at the Homestead in Virginia. It was shipped overseas to Egypt, Bermuda, Syria, Puerto Rico and Japan. Deute, the National executive, founded a society promoting fine food and beer. It had seventeen thousand members nationwide. A 1944 newspaper advertisement aimed at gourmet cooks claimed that it was the "ambition" of every Maine lobster to establish a friendly relationship with National Premium beer.

In 1946, when Hoffberger, the owner of the brewery and later owner of the Baltimore Orioles, flew to California with his wife, Alice, for their honeymoon, the well-known performer Victor Borge gave a party for the couple in Los Angeles, serving National Premium to the guests.

National beer patch. *Courtesy David Hoffberger.*

Above: Globe lights, like this one advertising National Premium, were given to tavern owners to attract customers. *Courtesy David Donovan Collection. Photo by Edward Brown.*

Left: Mr. Boh, Baltimore's unofficial mascot. *Courtesy David Hoffberger.*

A Satisfying History of Charm City Brewing

During World War II, when malt rationing put beer in short supply, the brewery told its followers, "If you can't find two bottles of National Premium be satisfied with one," adding the patriotic advice to "save your money and buy a war bond."

When metal beer bottle caps were in short supply during World War II, National and other Baltimore breweries distributed cloth bags to collect used caps. A customer who turned in a bag full of metal beer caps would get a prize, usually a pair of women's stockings.

Baltimore's other breweries fought for the market share as well. Globe published posters of its "Arrow Girls," images of scantily clad women, including a young Marilyn Monroe look-alike, that found their way to many ballroom walls. Gunther fought National hard, even though the Krieger clan, which owned Gunther, got along well with the Hoffbergers. Jerry Hoffberger's uncle, Harry, married Mollie Krieger.

In 1965, when William Kelley sent his voluminous *Brewing in Maryland* to press, he reported that National was humming along. Throughout the 1950s, National installed a new bottling line and considered doubling the size of its plant. However, the next decade ushered in dynamic changes in the beer business. Breweries had been largely regional enterprises because beer, like bread, grew stale when it traveled too far from its birthplace. Modernization and technological advances allowed breweries to increase their reach to distant markets, which altered the economics of selling beer. With the chance of a larger market within its grasp, a big brewery could freeze prices, drive out competition and rely on volume of sales to cover costs. At the same time, beer drinkers were migrating away from taverns, where local beers were served on tap, and sipping their six-packs at home. The large national breweries dominated take-home sales.

THE FADE

The trend came to a head in Baltimore as well. "The Small Breweries Are Disappearing" read a headline for a 1975 article in the *Sun*. Maryland-brewed beers accounted for 88 percent of the local market in 1955, and in 1974, they had dropped to 22 percent, the article noted.

In a vivid example of National's downturn, the brewery had to put its team of nineteen shire horses out to pasture in 1975. Acquired in 1972 as public relations competition for the Clydesdale of Anheuser-Busch, the shires were too expensive to keep, so the brewery outsourced them, sending some to equine operations in Idaho and others to a farm in Carroll County.

It was a scenario that was playing out in cities across America known for their traditions of brewing. In Philip van Munching's 1997 book *Beer Blastt*, he described how national breweries like Anheuser-Busch and Miller Brewing emerged as smaller regional breweries were swallowed. Peter Blum's 1999 *Brewed in Detroit* describes how Stroh Brewing Company stayed competitive for a while, even absorbing Schlitz, once the nation's leading brewer. But eventually the financial strains of price wars, lowered earnings and the debt incurred by the acquisition of G. Heileman (the brewery that had once swallowed National) forced Stroh to completely bow out of the beer business, selling to Pabst Brewing Company and Miller Brewing Company in April 1999.

Before it succumbed, National, like other regional breweries in the United States, fought incursions from much larger breweries in St. Louis and Milwaukee. National gave it a good effort and rallied for a time with an attention-grabbing campaign employing entertainers such as the comedian Redd Foxx and touting Colt 45 malt liquor as a "Completely Unique Experience." Because of its high alcohol content, close to 6 percent alcohol by volume, Colt 45 was a favorite of college fraternity boys, who dubbed it LPR, or liquid pants remover. But in the end, as has happened in so many other towns in America, the once dominant local brewery folded.

National's Farber recalled that in a late-night session at a brewers conference in 1960s, an executive of a large midwestern brewer warned him that it was coming to Baltimore and was "'going to price you out.' They couldn't market us out of business," Farber recalled, "but they could price us out."

Compounding the slide were some management decisions that, in hindsight, were not brilliant. The hallmark red label of National Bohemian was changed to white to make the beer appear to be lighter. "It was a pretty precipitous decline," Costello said in *Mr. Boh's Brewery*. "It all happened after the label change."

Another ill-fated decision was the introduction of four-packs of sixteen-ounce bottles, which like the new labels seemed to confuse Baltimore beer drinkers. The "Land of Pleasant Living" campaign was replaced with clunkers. One campaign touted National as being "brewed in the dark," while another claimed that National was "a beer to call your own." Meanwhile, the breweries based in Milwaukee and St. Louis unleashed saturation advertising campaigns that turned the heads and beer-drinking habits of Baltimore residents.

A Satisfying History of Charm City Brewing

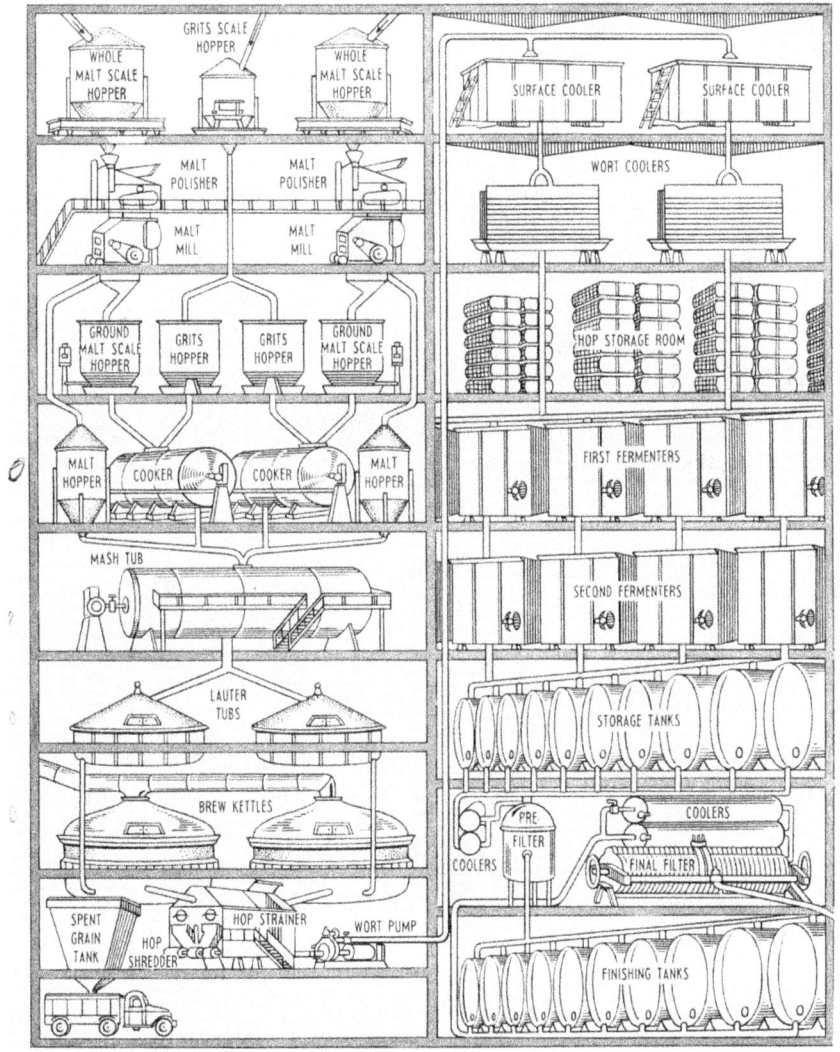

A diagram of the brewing process drawn in 1961 by National Brewing Company engineer Earl Seboda, showing how the process relies on the principle of gravity. *Courtesy Baltimore Museum of Industry.*

Over the years, National expanded and owned breweries in Baltimore, Miami, Phoenix and Detroit. But like countless other regional breweries, National faced the choice of spending more money and trying to grow or of getting out of the beer business.

The Hoffberger family, which over the years had run many enterprises, saw that the return on their investment in the brewery was fading. Baltimoreans,

Black Label was one of several beers made from 1960 to 1996 at the beltway brewery in Halethrope. Built by Carling in 1961, it was later operated as a joint venture between Carling and National, was taken over by G. Heileman and finally was bought by Stroh's, which closed it. *Courtesy the* Baltimore Sun.

once suspicious of out-of-towners, behaved like the rest of America, lapping up nationally advertised beers made in St. Louis and Milwaukee. In 1973, after consulting with family members, Jerry Hoffberger merged National Brewing Company with Carling. Hoffberger stayed on as the head of the merged operation for two more years before bowing out. The east Baltimore brewery was closed in 1978.

Carling National Breweries, which in 1960 had built a massive new brewery in Halethorpe, just off the Baltimore Beltway, took over National and focused all brewing at the beltway location. The merged operation was backed financially by Anton Rupert, a South African businessman. In 1979, the G. Heileman Brewing Company of LaCrosse, Wisconsin, bought the beltway brewery from Carling. National Premium and National Bohemian became just two more of the more than twenty canned beers occupying the "House of Heileman." But even high-flying Heileman, which in the 1980s had called itself "the envy of industry," failed. It was acquired in 1996 by Detroit's Stroh Brewing Company, which killed the once noble National Premium brand. Stroh, in turn, went out of business in 1999, selling the National Bohemian brand to Pabst Brewing Company.

A Satisfying History of Charm City Brewing

Bottling line of Carling Brewing Company. *Courtesy Baltimore Museum of Industry.*

In 1999, an attempt to revive National Premium drew a crowd, including former Maryland governor and Baltimore mayor William Donald Schaefer, to a kickoff event on the Baltimore waterfront. Mr. Schaefer, who at the time was state comptroller, took a celebratory sip of the brew, which he said he used to enjoy before he stopped drinking in 1968. However, production of National Premium failed to come to fruition when the brewer, Frederick Brewing Company, went into bankruptcy.

Meanwhile, Natty Bohemian, which had survived as a bargain beer, experienced a surge in popularity, especially with Baltimore's younger beer drinkers. Now brewed in Eden, North Carolina, at a MillerCoors plant, the light lager is being sold and distributed in Maryland by Pabst. The one-eyed "Mr. Boh" has become the unofficial mascot of the city. His image adorns

The large head of Mr. Boh. *Courtesy David Hoffberger.*

T-shirts and hats that are sold by Baltimore entrepreneur Todd Unger at his Natty Boh Gear shop in Fells Point and on his nattybohgear.com website. National Bohemian beer is poured on tap at the Oriole Park at Camden Yards for the princely sum of $7.50 per cup, a price that in earlier days would pay for a case of twenty-four cans.

National Premium is trying for a revival as well. Tim Miller, a realtor based in Easton, has bought the rights to National Premium, coaxed the recipe from a brewer who worked in the plant in the 1970s and has announced plans to resurrect the classic pilsner.

Gunther, Globe, Free State and American

The Other Post-Prohibition Breweries

While National Brewing Company reigned in Baltimore during the 1950s and '60s, it had spirited competition for the city's beer drinkers from the workers at Gunther, Globe, Free State and American. Here are their stories.

GUNTHER BREWING COMPANY

Gunther was one of the city's largest and oldest breweries and battled National, its east Baltimore neighbor, on many fronts, including tying its beer to the new baseball team in town, the Baltimore Orioles.

JoAnn Fruchtman, owner of the Children's Bookstore in Roland Park and an heir of Gunther executives, remembered a day in 1954 when she was a young girl wearing a brand-new turquoise leather jacket while she rode on a Gunther beer float along with her brother, Howard, in the parade that welcomed the baseball team to town. "We attended every opening day the brewery had box seats on the first baseline," Fruchtman said in a 2011 interview. "It was fun, and we got out of school."

Like its rivals, Gunther employed a stable of radio and television announcers, the most famous being Orioles announcers Ernie Harwell and Herb Carneal. Harwell and Carneal would occasionally dine at the home of Gunther's president, LeRoy "Lee" Cohen, Fruchtman's father. When the Yankees were in town, the men would bring along New York announcer Phil Rizzuto to the Cohen home on Long Meadow Road in Pikesville.

A scene from Conkling Street in 1936 showing steam rising from Gunther brewery. *Courtesy Baltimore Museum of Industry.*

Gunther announcers also broadcast the football games of the Baltimore Colts and the basketball games of the Baltimore Bullets. In 1952, when television was new and only a few programs were on the air, Gunther latched on to local sponsorship of the popular *Abbott and Costello* network comedy show that was aired Monday night on WBAL TV and supported the Gunther Premium Playhouse, which on Saturday nights showed first-run films like Claudette Colbert and Robert Cummings in *Sleep, My Love* on WMAR TV. Its spokesmen included Washington sportswriter Morrie Siegel, who had a show on WTOP TV in Washington, and newscaster Baxter Ward, who read the news and did commercials for Gunther on WBAL TV. Gunther even tapped ventriloquist Señor Wences and his two hand puppets, Johnny and Pedro, to plug the beer, with Pedro proclaiming in his signature deep voice that Gunther beer "is good."

Gunther signs lit up the city. The most spectacular was one near the city's main train terminal, Penn Station, at the corner of Lanvale and Charles Streets. There in a giant display of neon prowess, a glass of Gunther beer was poured into a tapered glass, while the time and temperature were shown.

A Satisfying History of Charm City Brewing

Massive Gunther electric billboard at Charles and Lanvale poured a beer and told the time and temperature in 1957. *Courtesy Howard Cohen.*

In another ploy, electric Gunther scoreboards dubbed "scorecasters" were installed at prominent spots around the area: Park Circle; St. Paul at the Orleans Street viaduct; Russell Street near Paca, Pratt and Calvert Streets; Pottee Street at Chesapeake Avenue; and in the 500 block of York Road in Towson. Wired to the WBAL radio studio, these seven-foot-tall boards would quickly relay the latest tallies of the Orioles and Colts games.

The brewery had a storied history. George Gunther Sr., a skilled brewer and cagey operator, assumed control of the brewery near Conkling and Dillion Streets in 1880 from Christian Gehl. Gehl was also a skilled brewer but spoke little English, and after he took a trip to his native Germany, he returned to Baltimore to find Gunther in charge of the brewery. The Gunther family lived in a twelve-room house near the brewery and operated a tavern on the first floor of the premises.

George Gunther also ruffled quite a few feathers in 1899 when he sold his brewery to the Maryland Brewing Company, the first beer trust. After serving as president of the trust, he finagled a way to set up his son, George Jr., in a new brewery, one that would be in direct competition with the trust. The trust sued, contending that this violated a no-competition clause, but the senior Gunther got away with the tactic, claiming that the new brewery was run by his son and not him.

The Gunther boys, George Jr. and Frank, were not the businessmen that their father was. One account has them losing $70,000 in a poker game to Colonel Jacob Ruppert, owner of Ruppert's Brewery in New York and the New York Yankees. The Gunther brewery had other problems as well, chief among them prohibition. The brewery stayed open during the Prohibition era, making a near beer, which was, by all accounts, pretty awful. They also made ice. In 1933, the business went into receivership, and Abraham Krieger, an officer of the Finance Company of America, took charge.

While Abraham Krieger did not care for beer, preferring the Baltimore Pure Rye whiskey made by other family members, the Gunther brewery had new life under his leadership. Air conditioning was installed in its new offices. The plant moved from steam power to electricity. And in perhaps his best management move, Krieger convinced his son-in-law, LeRoy S. Cohen, to join the brewery executive staff right after World War II. In 1949, the brewery installed ten forty-two-foot-long storage tanks, the biggest beer tanks in the city, according to an article in the *News-Post*. In 1950, Gunter got its back up, or got feisty. The brewery believed that the newly formed Wiessner Brewing Company Inc., successor to the Free State Brewing Corporation,

Though not quite health food, beer was once promoted as "healthful," as this Gunther advertisement shows. *Photo by Jim Burger.*

and a few New York breweries were making a beer that imitated Gunther's dry beer. Gunther ran large ads in newspapers proclaiming that Gunther was "the most imitated beer in the East…if not the whole USA." The ad went on to note that "most Maryland folks, we believe, would rather drink the original, famous, dry beer-y Gunther's than one of its recent imitations."

Things seemed to be going well in the late 1950s at Gunther. Cohen was named president of the brewery in 1954 at the age of thirty-six, making him the youngest head of a brewery in the United States. In 1956, the brewery opened a striking new three-story office building topped with a golden tower, symbolic of its popular Golden Brew beer. And in 1959, its new packaging line could process an amazing 1,650 bottles or cans per minute, quite an accomplishment. In Baltimore County, the sanitation workers who picked up the trash at the Cohen family home looked forward to their annual Christmas gift: cases of Gunther beer, wrapped in red bows, set out on the curb.

Yet the competition in the beer business was fierce. Cohen, the youthful leader of Gunther, had a heart attack in 1956 at the age of thirty-eight. He survived, but a few years later in December 1959, Gunther was sold to the Theo Hamm Brewing Company of St. Paul, Minnesota. At the time of the sale, Gunther workers gave Cohen a silver plaque thanking him for his years of leadership. He died three years later of another heart attack.

Hamm's, like many national breweries, was expanding, and it envisioned the Baltimore plant as a way to gain a foothold in the East Coast. Hamm's management made several moves that did not sit well with Gunther workers or with local beer drinkers. It purged the brewery tanks of all Gunther beer and initiated a massive cleaning operation of the brewery. It temporarily eliminated the Gunther brand, replacing it with Hamm's, a beer promoted by a dancing cartoon bear and a ditty that touted it as a beer from "the land of sky-blue waters." The beer drinkers of the Chesapeake Bay did not cotton to being told that Minnesota's waters were superior to those in the Land of Pleasant Living. Sales suffered.

Some brewery workers also felt that getting rid of all the Gunther beer put a curse on the new operation. Shortly after Hamm's took over, an explosion and fire in February 1960 killed two brewery workers who were putting a new glass lining in a beer tank. Then there is the story, perhaps apocryphal, of a train load of Hamm's beer that froze on its way from St. Paul to Baltimore. Eventually, the beer thawed and was served to Baltimore imbibers who, the story goes, turned up their noses, saying "nevermore" to the beer from Minnesota.

BALTIMORE BEER

Artist's rendering of the F. and M. Schaefer plant, which in 1963 took over the east Baltimore brewery from Theo Hamm Brewing Company, which had acquired it in 1959 earlier from Gunther Brewing Company. *Courtesy Baltimore Museum of Industry.*

Hamm's did try to resurrect the Gunther brand, bringing it back quietly in November 1962. But it was too late. In June 1963, about four years after it bought Gunther, Hamm's sold the Baltimore brewery to F. and M. Schaefer of New York. The New York brewery made a game effort and had a catchy slogan, saying that it was "the one beer to have when you are having more than one." It, too, tried to revive the Gunther brand. But in 1978, Schaefer gave up. In the following years, the old brewery had a variety of tenants, including for a time the city's noted horseradish maker, Tulkoff. The old Gunther brewery buildings are being renovated, turned into mixed-use units, including apartments, that no doubt will one day be occupied by a new generation of beer drinkers.

GLOBE BREWING COMPANY: MAKERS OF ARROW BEER AND SEXY POSTERS

Perhaps the feistiest brewing company that ever competed in the Baltimore market was Globe. Its building at the northeast corner of Hanover and Conway Streets was saved from the junk pile. Globe was held captive by two beer trusts that swallowed many Baltimore breweries, yet Globe escaped alive. It weathered prohibition. It used naked women to attract beer-drinking men to its Arrow beer. It disappeared in the mid-1960s, but not without a fight.

A Satisfying History of Charm City Brewing

Globe Brewery at Hanover and Conway Streets. News-American photo from Special Collections, University of Maryland Libraries, used with permission of Hearst Communications, Inc., Hearst Newspapers Division.

The brewery almost bit the dust in 1919. That was when the owners of Boston Iron & Metal Company, Morris Schapiro and John D. Roney, decided that rather than sell the building and fixtures for scrap, as they had done with many other breweries in their possession, they would keep Globe running as a brewery during prohibition. Globe made Arrow Special, a near beer with less than 0.5 percent alcohol.

When beer again became legal, Globe's brewer, John J. Fitzgerald, was ready to make the switch to approved suds, producing the first legal post-prohibition beer in Maryland. At midnight on April 7, 1933, crowds jammed the bar of the Hotel Rennert in downtown Baltimore, where among the parched was H.L. Mencken, who sipped an Arrow beer and proclaimed that it was "pretty good, not bad at all."

Starting in 1940s and continuing into the early 1960s, Globe used sex—striking pinups of nude women—to lure customers to its brews.

Each nude was given a name, such as "Matchless Body," a play on words that could also apply to Arrow beer. These pinups, which probably were first used in calendars and then repurposed for Globe ads, were the work of two commercial artists. One was Earl Moran, who in the 1940s hired a model named Norma Jeane Dougherty, later known as Marilyn Monroe, to pose for him in his California studio. David Donovan, a Baltimore collector of these works, speculates that the Arrow beer print called "Perfection" might have used Monroe as its model. The other artist was a woman, Zoe Mozart, who often posed for her own paintings, using mirrors and cameras to capture the pose and then painting the pinup from the photo.

Appealing to the prurient interest of men, the traditional beer-drinking target market, had long been a tactic of beer advertising, observed Larry Handy, vice-president of the East Coast Breweriana Association. Writing in the winter 2006 issue of *The Keg*, the association's publication, Hardy said that "some of the earliest commercially produced advertising in this country featured attractive and partially clothed women on trays, lithographed prints and calendars." But what distinguished the Arrow prints was the use of complete nudity, he wrote. While to today's eyes, the prints have an artistic, if racy, allure, by the standards of the 1940s, when they first appeared, they were, Handy said, "rare and bordering on scandalous."

But the Arrow nudes sold beer, and in the rough-and-tumble rivalry of Baltimore's beer market, Globe could use the help. It tried a variety of tactics. Shortly after its brewmaster, Fitzgerald, who was known for his hoppy Shamrock Ale, died in the mid-1940s, the brewery switched from ales to lagers. Its Imperial Arrow Lager sold well for a while, as did its Arrow 77 pilsner. A brew called Hals, modeled after a full-bodied Dutch beer and using the image of *The Laughing Cavalier*, a painting by Dutch artist Franz Hals, briefly tasted success. From time to time, a man dressed as a cavalier would appear in Baltimore saloons, buying rounds for the assembled patrons.

Globe had impressive historical roots. The brewery was built in 1816 by Captain Joseph Leonard, a fabled Baltimore brewer who could trace his beer-making lineage back to Baltimore's first brewery, Barnitz. In subsequent years, Globe went through almost fifteen different incarnations and ownerships. It was one of the few Baltimore breweries to survive after it entered into the two beer trusts—Maryland Brewing Company and Gottleib-Bauernschmidt-Straus. It weathered prohibition. Yet by the early 1960s, it was in trouble, and in August 1963, Globe stopped brewing beer

A Satisfying History of Charm City Brewing

in Baltimore. The company transferred beer-making operations to the Cumberland Brewing Company. Its quite diminished Baltimore staff was reduced to merely distributing Arrow beer.

In 1965, the big brick Globe building, site of much history and beer making, was demolished to make room for a parking lot.

Free State: A Beer Named by a Newspaperman

After prohibition, the return of legal beer gave birth to a new brewery, Free State. This building, at 1108 Hillen, had a sudsy legacy, serving over the years both as the Frederick Bauernschmidt brewery and, later, as the American Malt Company.

Tray for Free State, a beer made after prohibition. The beer took its name from a phrase penned by *Baltimore Sun* editorial writer Hamilton Owens, who noted that the state was reluctant to enforce federal liquor laws. *Courtesy David Donovan Collection. Photo by Edward Brown.*

The brewery "will hum again," an advertisement in the *Sun* promised in May 1933. A member of the Bauernschmidt clan, Fred, was on the Free State Board, and its first brewer, John Merzbacher Sr., had worked at Gunther. Because of his technical skill, Merzbacher was known throughout the brewing industry as "the brewing doctor."

The name of the brewery, Free State, came from the title that *Evening Sun* editorial writer Hamilton Owens bestowed on Maryland because of its reluctance to hire state agents to enforce prohibition. Free State proved to be a popular beer, helped along by the practice of local saloons to sell glasses of draft Free State for a nickel. Free State lasted seventeen years, going out of business on May 26, 1950.

Three days later came an announcement that another brewery, this one called the Wiessner Brewing Company Inc., was taking over the Free State plant and would brew beer. The Wiessner name came from the German family with a long brewing tradition in Baltimore, but the man who ran the operation was Morton T. Sarubin. Sarubin also operated a clothing store, the Regal Shop, on West Baltimore Street, and the beer produced by his brewery was dubbed Regal.

Regal was not a hit, and this brewery did not last long. Two years after it began operations, this brewery known as the "lesser Wiessner" went into receivership, and it closed in the summer of 1952. A building on the southeast corner of Greenmount Avenue and Monument Street that the brewery owned was converted to a warehouse for an electrical supply company in 1956. Now that building is vacant.

American Brewery: A Beauty Still Standing

If you had to pick one building that told of the grandeur of old Baltimore breweries, it would be the architectural gem that stands on 1700 block of North Gay Street, a structure known to most Baltimoreans as the old American Brewery.

Built in 1887 for John F. Wiessner, the structure was one of the largest pre-prohibition breweries in the city, producing a remarkable 100,000 barrels of beer per year. It is also an architectural wonder, with brick archways, graceful round windows and a dramatic tower that soars some 140 feet toward the sky.

It offers a commanding view of Baltimore, and looking out from its windows, it is not hard to think back to Wiessner's era, when brewery workers

A Satisfying History of Charm City Brewing

American Beer's post–World War II bathing beauty poster. *Courtesy David Donovan Collection. Photo by Edward Brown.*

lived across Gay Street and when Wiessner and his fellow Germans gathered in the nearby Schuetzen Park, one of several in the city, for afternoons of picnicking, bowling, dancing and marksmanship contests.

Wiessner was a highly successful, if opinionated, brewer. Not only did he refuse to join the beer trusts that were swallowing up many of the city's breweries at the turn of the century, he also warred against them, keeping his highly regarded beer some fifty cents per barrel cheaper than those offered by the trusts.

His brewery building, full of idiosyncratic wonders, was graced by a metal statue of Gambrinus, the bearded and jolly patron saint of beer. Beer in hand, Gambrinus now smiles upon visitors at his new home, the Maryland Historical Society.

In 1931, some eleven years after prohibition stopped Wiesser's beer making, the building was taken over by the American Malt Company. Its product, a hop-flavored malt syrup that could be used by home brewers, was in great demand. Under the direction of John L. FitzSimons, the malt operation flourished and, foreseeing the end of prohibition, began to ready the plant to yield beer as well as malt syrup. By July 1933, a few short months after repeal, the brewery began selling American Pilsener, a beer with labels wrapped in the patriotic colors of red, white and blue. Sales zoomed, and shareholders were paid a 32 percent dividend over three years. In the 1940s, the brewery quit making malt and added an expensive but massive canning line, churning out record numbers of seven-ounce cone-shaped cans of beer.

Riding high in the 1950s, the brewery garnered a gold medal from the Brewers Association of America. The plant purchased an electronic device

Left: A statue of Gambrinus, known as both the king and patron saint of beer, standing outside the American Brewery. Now he resides at the Maryland Historical Society. *Courtesy Baltimore Museum of Industry*.

Below: Arrow beer tray depicting Gambrinus, the king of beer, celebrating the end of prohibition as a dour Mr. Volstead, seated in chair, looks on. *Courtesy David Donovan Collection. Photo by Edward Brown.*

A Satisfying History of Charm City Brewing

from RCA (the first in the industry) that detected foreign matter in the beer and alerted when vessels on the bottling line were either too full or short of beer. Even with the modern equipment, there were mishaps, such as the one in the summer of 1956 when a batch of bad beer had to be tossed out at a cost of $4,500.

Keeping with its patriotic theme, the brewery hired Jane Ward Murray, a dance teacher at Peabody Institute and Goucher College, to dress in Native American garb and appear as the "Indian Girl" in a series of advertisements.

American tried to compete by getting bigger, swallowing Pittsburgh's Fort Pitt Brewing Company. But in 1973, faced by strong competition from national brands like Schlitz and Budweiser, as well as the local breweries National and Schaeffer, American closed.

The brewery has been restored to much of its former glory. When the building was reopened in 2008, C. William Struever, whose firm did the renovation, described the structure as "simply breathtaking." The chief tenant of the building is Humanim, a nonprofit that provides job training and clinical support for children and adults with developmental and behavioral disabilities. Many of the brewery's fixtures have been retained and reworked. Sections of an old metal storage tank, for instance, now serve as a computer station.

The soaring spaces of the old American Brewery have been cleverly transformed into thirty-two thousand square feet for modern offices and community functions. Despite these touches, the building retains unique old-world grandeur. The American Brewery is, as the *Sun*'s Jacques Kelly wrote at its reopening, a "temple to malt and hops."

Advertising

It's All in the Jingle

"Tastes Great, Less Filling." The Budweiser Clydesdales. A crystalline stream flowing through the Rockies. Beer lovers identify with their favorite brews because of their commercials as much as their flavors. Two high-water marks of television advertising for Baltimore breweries included the "Land of Pleasant Living" campaign for National Bohemian and the "Completely Unique Experience" spots promoting Colt 45 malt liquor.

The "Land of Pleasant Living" campaign featured a series of animated characters, such as a chorus of singing clams, a melodious troubadour and a beer-toting pelican. These characters roamed the Chesapeake Bay recounting tales of local history, touting the benefits of living in the region and singing the praises of National beer, which, as the jingle reminded, was "brewed on the shores of the Chesapeake Bay." The ads captured the attention of Baltimore and remain part of the city's collective history. Even today the sounds of singing shellfish stir memories.

The Colt 45 television commercials depicted a fashionably dressed man acting blasé as life's extremes—a raging bull, a roaring waterfall, beautiful women and piano-playing gorillas—swirl around him. The coat-and-tie leading man, played by actor Billy Van, perks up only when presented with a glass of Colt 45. The eighteen spots highlighted danger, humor and a tagline that most of Baltimore could soon recite from memory: "In the dull and commonplace occurrences of day-to-day living, one thing stands out as a completely unique experience, Colt 45 Malt Liquor."

While certainly popular in Baltimore, some of the Colt 45 commercials went on to capture widespread acclaim. A sixty-second spot called "Machine,"

A Satisfying History of Charm City Brewing

Troubadour cartoon character used in the popular National "Land of Pleasant Living" advertising campaign. *Courtesy David Hoffberger.*

which employed an elaborate Rube Goldberg–like contraption to pour a glass of malt liquor, was selected by New York's Metropolitan Museum of Art as a masterpiece of man and machine on film. "Beach," in which Van waits for his malt liquor as a platoon of machine gun–firing soldiers (actually lads from Hofstra University's ROTC program) secure a beach head, won a Clio Award—the Oscars of advertising—for best beer or wine commercial of 1966. It rarely aired, however, because at the time network news brought the horror of real warfare in Vietnam into America's living rooms. The brewery pulled the "Beach" spot after receiving complaints from relatives of soldiers.

"Land of Pleasant Living"

Both the Colt 45 and National beer campaigns sprang from creative minds at the W.B. Doner agency. In fact, to land the account, the Detroit-based agency agreed to set up an office in town. So, in 1955, Brod Doner sent a young account executive named Herb Fried eastward to set up shop in Baltimore (where W.B. Doner eventually became one of the city's largest ad agencies). "It was a nice piece of business, $3 to $4 million dollars," Fried recalled. "Beer campaigns made this agency."

Top left: Cartoon bird character used in National's "Land of Pleasant Living" advertising campaign. *Courtesy David Hoffberger.*

Top right: Cartoon pelican character used in National's "Land of Pleasant Living" beer campaign. *Courtesy David Hoffberger.*

Left: Cartoon turtle used in the "Land of Pleasant Living" campaign. *Courtesy David Hoffberger.*

Chipper and still working in his mid-eighties, Fried described the relationship between the Doner agency and Hoffberger as "unique in the world of advertising." Building on reminiscences he offered in the late 1990s, Fried said in a 2012 interview that Hoffberger "never tried to fire us and was willing to experiment."

Doner eventually closed its Baltimore operation in 2003, but one morning years earlier, Fried sat in his Inner Harbor office viewing a videotape of the "Land of Pleasant Living" spots. "It was great campaign," Fried said as he watched the antics of an animated troubadour and singing clams. A Doner secretary who caught a glimpse of the tape nodded knowingly and reported, "Those are still my father's favorite commercials."

Several stories abound regarding how the "Land of Pleasant Living" campaign got its name. One story related by Baltimore writer Gilbert Sandler in an August 6, 1991 column in the Baltimore *Evening Sun* chronicled how Jerry Hoffberger, brewery owner and also owner of the Orioles, recalled a particular airplane ride over the Chesapeake Bay. "Early in the 1950s," Gilbert quoted Hoffberger, "several executives and I from National, Brod Doner and Herb Fried from our advertising agency had just taken off in a plane from Harbor Field, and I remember looking out over the bay. It was a brilliant, sunlit day, and I couldn't help saying, 'What a gorgeous sight!' Doner picked up on that and he said, quite extemporaneously, 'This is the land of pleasant living.'"

Other tales of the fateful plane trip tell of someone looking out over the bay and uttering, "Oh, what a mud hole!" But Fried backed Sandler's account of Hoffberger's exuberance and Doner's prophetic reply.

Hamm's Bear

Another factor that figured in the birth of the "Land of Pleasant Living" campaign was the arrival of Hamm's bear in Baltimore. In 1959, the Theo Hamm Brewing Company of St. Paul, Minnesota, bought the old Gunther brewery across O'Donnell Street from National in east Baltimore and looked to grab some of the local market. Hamm's ad campaign featured an animated dancing bear and a jingle touting the beer as being "from the land of sky-blue waters."

A joke that circulated among beer drinkers and brewers at the time asked, "What separated the land of pleasant living from the land of sky-blue waters?" The answer, of course, was "O'Donnell Street."

Hamm's foray into the Baltimore market caught the attention of officials at National. According to Bill Costello, head of advertising for National from 1964 to 1974, the Baltimore brewery began looking for a campaign to counter Hamm's dancing bear. Using animated characters in beer commercials was a relatively new idea. When executives at National warmed to the concept of cartoon characters pitching their beer, they turned to Doner, who selected the animation shop of Stan Walsh, Quartet Films in Los Angeles, to literally draw up specifics. Walsh was perched atop the class of the emerging animated advertising group that had created Tony the Tiger and the Jolly Green Giant. Walsh and Quartet Films had also created the Hamm's bear.

What the animators at Quartet Films created delighted the folks at National. A series of cartoon characters—troubadour, pelican, turtle, dive-bombing ducks and even Lord Calvert—recounted highlights of local history and sang of the glories of living on the Chesapeake Bay. The voices of the characters were provided by Mel Blanc, Candy Candido and singer Hamilton Camp. The smart campaign, catchy lyrics by noted songwriter Henry Russell and hometown themes reinforced local pride. One spot recounted the brewing history of Baltimore, while in another the turtle and a bird toting a vacuum cleaner discourage littering.

The "Land of Pleasant Living" spots sent the Hamm's bear into hibernation. After the campaign ran for four years, from 1959 to 1963, Hamm's sold its

Cartoon clam used in the "Land of Pleasant Living" campaign. *Courtesy David Hoffberger.*

east Baltimore plant to F. and M. Schaefer Brewing Company. The "Land of Pleasant Living" outlasted the land of sky-blue waters.

National Bohemian benefited from another clever cartoon campaign called "Draw One," spots in which an artistic character sketches glasses of beer. Then there was a rousing television commercial featuring singer-songwriter Valerie Simpson. Sporting an impressive Afro hairstyle popular in the 1970s, she strolled through Baltimore praising the town and its beers—or, as she put it, "Me and Boh go hand in hand." The spot was so popular that when Simpson appeared onstage at the Baltimore City Fair in the 1970s, the audience begged her to "sing the commercial." She did and got a rousing ovation.

Colt 45: "Completely Unique Experience"

In early 1960s, when sales of National Bohemian started to slip due to the incursion by Anheuser-Busch and Miller brewing companies, Colt 45 malt liquor sprang to life. The new brew provided National with a fresh revenue stream. It also produced a distinctive, hilarious television advertising campaign. Don Schnably was one of the Doner crew who dreamed up the storylines for the commercial. Costello, who supervised the shoots for National, and Billy Van, the Canadian actor who starred in the spots, were two of the players in the team of National and Doner of creative minds that pushed the campaign's success.

Costello explained that National began brewing Colt 45 to placate distributors in the Southeast. Unlike the present system, in which beer distributors handle the products of several breweries, wholesalers in 1963 for the most part were tied to one domestic brewer. While National Bohemian controlled most of the Maryland market, the introduction of bargain beers Old Milwaukee by Schlitz and Busch Bavarian by Anheuser-Busch hurt sales of National Bohemian in other regions of the country, especially the Southeast. At the time, National had three breweries, one each in Baltimore, Miami and Detroit. (It later bought another one in Phoenix to brew Colt 45 for the western market.)

Since National Bohemian was not selling well in the Southeast, distributors there asked National to either develop a new product or allow them to carry another brand of beer on their trucks. The latter was never an option, so National came up with the new product: a malt liquor (lager brewed to be higher in alcohol). The name "malt liquor" stems from the fact that some states prohibit a brew with an alcohol content of 5.5 percent by volume or higher to be called "beer."

The national scene boasted only one other significant malt liquor, Country Club made by Goetz Brewing Company in St. Joseph, Missouri, so the beer barons at National launched their own, naming it Colt 45. The name conveyed the powerful beverage's wallop while artfully dodging association with the similarly named pistol by omitting the period before "45." A popular local football team also went by the name Colts, and National took every opportunity to reinforce the connection. The team's logo, a Colt jumping through goalposts, was mirrored by the malt liquor label, which replaced the goal posts with a horseshoe. National also produced a seven-ounce bottle of beer called Colt in the late 1950s and early 1960s to capitalize on the football team's success. The small bottles of Colt particularly appealed to ladies, thousands of whom were Baltimore Colts fans. The brewery paid a royalty to the Colts football team for use of the Colt 45 logo. Linking the brew to the football team, not the revolver of the same name, eased it past federal regulations that prohibit a beer being named after a firearm.

The first batch of Colt 45 was made in the Miami brewery and shipped to stores in the surrounding area. Sales took off, with many distributors selling out, oddly enough, in the first forty-five days. Various sorts of beer drinkers enjoyed this affordable brew, but it sold especially well on college campuses.

To push sales higher, National instructed the Doner group to develop television ads. A classic advertising campaign emerged: eighteen spots built on the theme of a smooth character unfazed by the world around him, sparking to life only when crossing paths with a Colt 45. The commercials included few words, often containing just sixteen seconds of "ad copy" during the sixty-second spot and an announcer's voice closing with the memorable "Completely Unique Experience" tagline.

The commercials relied on strong, often elaborately contrived, visual images—man threatened by raging bull, man threatened by shark or man threatened by falling tree—and distinctive music, such as "Solfaggio." Copped from an obscure George Gershwin tune, "Solfaggio" was widely remembered as the theme from a television skit featuring a three-gorilla band led by comedian Ernie Kovacs. After Kovacs died in a 1962 automobile accident, Costello flew to Las Vegas to negotiate with his widow, performer Edie Adams, over royalty payments for turning the gorilla band theme into a beer commercial. She not only agreed but also insisted that she appear in the spot. So Edie Adams dressed in a gorilla suit and played the piano while her musical colleagues monkeyed around.

A Satisfying History of Charm City Brewing

Edie Adams and Redd Foxx

In addition to Edie Adams, another big-name performer who appeared in a Colt 45 commercial was Redd Foxx. The idea was hatched at a Hollywood party. Billy Van had moved to California from Canada after landing a role on *The Sonny & Cher Comedy Hour*. Foxx spotted Van at the party, recognized him as "the guy in Colt ads" and told Van that he loved the commercials. Van passed the word along to Costello during one of their regular long-distance telephone chats with his Baltimore friend. Costello leaped at the opening. Foxx was a nationally known television star, with *Sanford and Son* at the top of the Nielsen ratings. Costello had been looking for a famous black entertainer to use in the commercials to reinforce the brew's popularity in African American communities.

But could National afford Redd Foxx? Over in the brewery's east Baltimore office, Costello got the brewery's chief administrative officer, Dawson Farber, to approve spending up to $100,000. A few days later in New York, Costello held his breath after asking Foxx's lawyer, Jimmy Tolbert, what it would cost to get Foxx in one commercial. The lawyer replied that the fee would be $20,000. Foxx later told Costello that Baltimore held a fond spot in his heart. The comedian appeared many times in Pennsylvania Avenue nightspots like the Royal Theater, and unlike what happened in some other cities, Foxx had always been paid in Baltimore.

Filming the Colt 45 commercials presented many physical dangers. Foxx ended up appearing in two Colt 45 commercials. One, called "Hotel," showed the front of hotel—actually a set on a Twentieth Century Fox back lot in Hollywood—collapse, narrowly missing Foxx and Van. Foxx cracked, "That's urban renewal for ya." The commercial was shot in one take. Foxx also appeared in the last of the "Completely Unique Experience" series, a spot called "Ski Jump." A car, presumably driven by Foxx, flies off a ski jump and delivers the Colt 45 to a skiing beauty, who pours it for Van. It was deemed so dangerous that at the last minute, the stuntman who was supposed to drive the car backed down, so a dummy was propped up in the driver's seat and crew members let the car slide down the ski jump. Much to the amazement of all concerned, the soaring car made a perfect landing at the bottom of the hill.

Van contended that while often uneasy during the filming of these commercials, he was rarely afraid. However, Van recalled that he was somewhat shaken in the wilds of Oregon when a stuntman walking on a tightrope almost fell into raging waters. He remembered feeling uneasy in

Arecibo, Puerto Rico, when during filming a twin-engine aircraft took off a few feet above his head. Van prompted the director to order the plane to buzz him again; it ended up taking four takes to get the shot right. Then there was the time he almost drowned in a Long Island swimming pool, filming the "Underwater" spot, when his oxygen hose got tangled with the underwater camera. A well-muscled member of the film crew came to his rescue, quickly pulling Van to the surface.

But compared to what happened to Van's stand-in during the "Bullfight" spot, Van said that he felt lucky. Filmed in a bullring at a mountaintop Mexican estate, this spot originally called for Van to sit at a table while the bull and matador tussle a few feet away. Because of the scene's obvious danger, another matador with the same build as Van stood in for the actor and wore one of Van's extra suits. The substitute, whom Van knew only as "Juan," loved the suit and repeatedly asked if he could keep it. Van replied that he did not have the authority to give away the threads, but the bull changed all that. Rather than following the movements of the matador's cape, the bull suddenly charged the table where Juan sat. A flapping edge of the tablecloth caught the bull's attention, and with cameras rolling, it plowed into the table, knocking Van's stand-in to the ground. The fiberglass table shielded the poor matador from being gored and seriously injured, but Juan ended up getting Van's suit. Later, back in New York, some quick studio shots made it seem that after being run over by the bull, Van sat down and took a long sip of a Colt 45.

American Beer Indian Girl

Meanwhile, other Baltimore breweries mounted memorable advertising campaigns. In the late 1950s, American Brewery came up with the "American Beer Indian Girl," who wore Native American garb and danced to an American beer jingle. She was a sensation, appearing in print advertisements and on billboards around town. The Indian Girl, Jane Ward Murray, was an accomplished performer who taught ballet at the Peabody Institute and Goucher College and was married to a federal judge, Herbert F. Murray. Both are deceased.

American also sponsored fishing contests, awarding prizes from $5 to $25,000 to fisherman who reeled in tagged fish set loose in Lake Roland, the Loch Raven reservoir and the Chesapeake Bay. William Simmons, a longshoremen, reeled in the $25,000 striped bass dubbed Diamond Jim III

A Satisfying History of Charm City Brewing

Ever mindful of the goodwill of bartenders and a chance for free advertising, Baltimore breweries provided tip jars to local establishments. *Photo by Jim Burger.*

Pretty girls sell beer, and Free State had this saucy redhead in one of its advertisements. *Courtesy David Donovan Collection. Photo by Edward Brown.*

in 1958; he also landed some tax troubles. In federal court a few years later, Simmons argued that catching the fish was a civic achievement and that he was therefore exempt from paying federal tax on the money. The judge was amused by the plea but ruled that Simmons owed the government $6,230.

Globe Brewery was known for its "Laughing Cavalier" character. A painting of the cavalier by artist Frans Hals appeared on the label of the beer, while a man dressed as the Cavalier appeared at bibulous events around Baltimore, often arriving in a horse-drawn coach.

Even though National Bohemian and Colt 45 have faded, their old ad campaigns remain examples of brilliant work. "This was a conservative, blue-collar town," Costello said, "and the 'Land of Pleasant Living' campaign appealed to regional pride. In content, animation, tune and lyrics, it was up there. If it had been a national campaign, it would be in the history books of advertising."

The Colt 45 campaign succeeded for two reasons, in Costello's estimation. First, there was the demeanor of Billy Van, the actor picked for the job by National's then director of advertising, Frank Cashen (before Cashen jumped from the beer business to the baseball business). "People would come up to me and say, 'That Colt 45 guy is so cool,'" said Costello. "That word kept coming up." The strong, familiar theme music also proved crucial. "You could be two rooms away, hear that music on the TV and know what commercial was on." Summing up the experience of working at National, the brewery with two exceptional ad campaigns, Costello said, "It was not the best-paying job I ever had, but it was the best job I ever had."

Doner continued to be the advertising agency for National even as its ownership changed from Carling to G. Heileman. But in the minds of many Baltimoreans, the "Land of Pleasant Living" and Colt 45 "Completely Unique Experience" campaigns have never been equaled.

Sports and Beer

The classic combination of beer and sports has been as much a part of Baltimore's collective memory as the image of the Colts' Alan Ameche bulldozing across the goal line in 1958 to defeat the New York Giants for the National Football League Championship in "the greatest game ever played." Consider some of the city's beery sports highlights.

- In the 1890s, the Von der Horst family owned a local baseball team, the American Association Orioles, and a local brewery, the Eagle Brewery and malt works. The Orioles went on to join the National League and play at Union Field at Twenty-fifth and Barclay Streets; they won the pennant three straight years and the championship series in 1896 and 1897.

- Decades later, a scoreboard advertising Gunther beer graced the old Oriole Park on what is now Twenty-ninth and Greenmount Avenue and even survived the 1944 fire that destroyed the ball yard.

- In 1948, four of the city's reigning beer royalty—Zanvyl Krieger, whose family ran Gunther; Sam Hoffberger, whose family ran National; Arrow's Francis McNamara; and American's Leiter FitzSimons—played prominent roles in a "Save the Colts" drive that kept the club from going belly up.

- Jerry Hoffberger, who ran National Brewing Company and eventually ended up owning the Orioles as well, teamed up with

Jerry Hoffberger, owner of National Brewing Company and the Baltimore Orioles, with manager Earl Weaver. *Courtesy David Hoffberger.*

the beer barons at Gunther to play crucial roles in bringing the Orioles to Baltimore in 1954.

- Once the teams were here, the breweries fought over putting their name on the scoreboards. National beer got the prime advertising spot on the center field scoreboard in 1970 at the old Memorial Stadium, but only after it had been occupied by rivals Gunther, Hamm's and Schaefer.

- During his playing days, former Oriole slugger John "Boog" Powell not only enjoyed the perk of playing for a team run by a man who owned National brewery, but he also stayed on the beer bandwagon in retirement. He, along with other former athletes and umpires and "a babe," appeared in Miller Lite's wildly successful "Tastes Great, Less Filling" television ad campaigns. "In the world of video art, they are Dutch miniatures," wrote Frank DeFord, a Baltimore native, in *Lite Reading*, a book he authored chronicling the effect of these beer commercials.

- At the start of the 2011 baseball season, local beer drinkers rejoiced when National Bohemian, a beer with Baltimore roots that is now brewed in Eden, North Carolina, had a homecoming, returning to the taps in the Orioles ballpark.

BEER BARONS AND A SILVER BULLET BRING BASEBALL TO BALTIMORE

The tale of how the beer barons, with the help of a silver bullet, worked to bring the Orioles to Baltimore has not often been told. One day in his Towson home, Dawson Farber, a former executive at National Brewing Company who died in 2007, told the story.

Hoffberger, owner of National Brewing Company, was one of a group of Baltimore businessmen that wanted to bring the St. Louis Browns to town in 1954. At the time, Hoffberger had a limited knowledge of baseball. So he took Farber—his aide who had played high school baseball at Gilman, a private school in Baltimore, and in college at Princeton University—with him to meet with Browns owner Bill Veeck at the St. Louis ballpark. Before the game, Farber huddled with Hoffberger, briefing him on the St. Louis team and its players. After sitting through the game talking baseball with Hoffberger, Veeck took a liking to the Baltimore beer man. The deal was off to a good start.

Executives at the Gunther brewery also played a big role putting together the money to secure the Orioles and, along with Clarence Miles, James Keelty Jr. and Joseph A.W. Inglehart, lined up an ownership group to bring the team to town.

But before an umpire could holler, "Play ball!" in Baltimore, the Washington Senators had to say okay. According to the business practices of major-league baseball, no team could move within fifty miles of an existing franchise without the approval of the owner of the existing franchise. This meant that Clark Griffith, owner of the Washington Senators, some thirty miles south of Baltimore, had to agree. This was where the silver bullet came into play.

Hoffberger dispatched Farber to Washington to lay the groundwork for a deal. During one of his visits with Griffith, Farber noticed that Griffith was a huge fan of *The Lone Ranger* radio show. When Griffith's birthday,

Breweries promoted moving the Orioles to Baltimore from St. Louis, as shown by this 1954 article from *The Good Word*, an in-house Gunther publication. *Courtesy Howard Cohen.*

November 20, rolled around, Farber sent him a silver bullet, the Lone Ranger's trademark. Griffith appreciated the gesture and soon was ready to make an arrangement with the Baltimore brewer. Griffith agreed to let the Orioles set up shop in Baltimore. In return, Hoffberger's National Brewing Company agreed to sponsor television broadcasts of Griffith's Washington Senators games. In short, beer and a bullet brought baseball to Baltimore.

BROADCASTERS WHO POURED BEER

This was a time when sports broadcasters worked not for the team or a network but for a brewery. Chuck Thompson served not only as the voice of the Orioles baseball games but also as the "voice" of National beer. A gregarious man known for his signature phrase, "Ain't the beer cold!" became known around Baltimore as an expression of joy. It is also the title of his biography. Thompson, a winner of the Ford C. Frick Award from the National Baseball Hall of Fame, spoke about his work with Baltimore breweries in an interview conducted in his northern Baltimore County home a few years before his

A Satisfying History of Charm City Brewing

death in March 2005. Thompson laughed as he recalled his duties of reading beer commercials between innings and, in the off-season, appearing at civic gatherings as a representative of National Brewing Company.

One indication of the spirited competition between breweries could be found in the sports reports of local broadcaster and sometime professional football player Nick Campofreda, whose broadcasts were sponsored by American Brewery. When Campofreda reported baseball scores, he refused to say "National League." That would be mentioning the name of a competing brewery. Instead, he called it the "senior circuit." As a native of Baltimore who played football at Western Maryland (now McDaniel) College and for the Washington Redskins, Campofreda cut quite a figure in Baltimore.

"High school hockey used to be big in Baltimore, and Nick Campofreda would be at all games and walk through the crowd," according to Turkey Joe Trabert, a Baltimore native who was in high school in the early 1950s. "There was a rink on North Avenue near St. Paul Street, and on Friday nights they sold American beer at the hockey games. With Nick Campofreda there and a crowd—that was as big as it got," Trabert added. Campofreda had another memorable feature. "He was bald and had a terrible, terrible wig," Trabert noted.

Ernie Harwell's voice belonged to Gunther at least during the seasons when Gunther sponsored the broadcast of the Baltimore Colts games. "When the extra point sailed through the uprights, I would say, 'It is good like Gunther's,'" Harwell recalled in a 2005 interview five years before his death. Harwell broadcast the Orioles games from 1954 to 1959 and was well known around town. A regular visitor to Harwell's Blythewood Road farmhouse was a skinny eighteen-year-old player, Brooks Robinson, who would drop by the house to play catch with Harwell's sons.

Gunther also dispatched Harwell to civic gatherings around Baltimore. "I would show game films and answer questions," Harwell said, adding that sometimes the local groups he spoke to were not entirely sure who he was or why they had invited him. They simply knew that if they telephoned the brewery, it would provide free entertainment. "We used to say if they couldn't find a fan dancer, they would send us out," Harwell said.

Harwell and his fellow announcer Herb Carneal would occasionally dine at the home of Gunther's president LeRoy "Lee" Cohen. When the Yankees were in town, the men would bring along New York announcer Phil Rizzuto to the Cohen home on Long Meadow Road in Pikesville.

The Krieger family had deep ties to the Colts. Zanvyl Krieger, a prominent attorney, had been on the team's board of directors since the 1940s. When the team was sold back to the NFL in the 1950s, Krieger sued the league, an action that resulted in the Colts returning to Baltimore in 1953. The Gunther brewery, an enterprise run by LeRoy Cohen, a Krieger in-law, jousted with National and other local breweries to ally itself with the Colts. National tied its logo to team pictures and sponsored *Corralin' the Colts*, a television program that featured Colt players recounting the team's latest game. Popular with Baltimore viewers, the show seemed to have a limited effect on changing the beer-drinking preferences of some of the players.

John Steadman, longtime sports columnist for the *News-American* and later the *Baltimore Sun* and who died in 2001, recalled that a favorite ploy of Colts who had appeared on National's *Corralin' the Colts* was to show up at area taverns and ask for a competitor's beer. "Bill Pellington, the linebacker, used to show up at the Iron Horse in Lutherville after the show and say, 'Gimme a Schlitz,'" Steadman said in an 2000 interview, "and Artie Donovan only drank Schlitz, and only from a can."

National put together a network of East Coast television stations that broadcast Colts games, but according to Frank Cashen, it folded when the National Football League assumed broadcast rights to all games. In his career in Baltimore, Cashen worked for Hoffberger at National Brewing Company, where he was head of advertising, and then with the Baltimore Orioles, for whom he was executive vice-president of baseball operations. Shortly after he had settled into the Oriole front office, the team won the 1966 World Series, sweeping the Los Angeles Dodgers, with star pitchers Sandy Koufax and Don Drysdale, in four games. Cashen, however, took little credit for the sweep, saying in a 2011 interview that the championship team was largely built by Lee MacPhail and Harry Dalton, the team's general managers. Cashen briefly returned to the brewery at Hoffberger's request. But when the brewery was sold to Carling, Cashen took another baseball job as general manager for the New York Mets and was widely credited for assembling the World Championship 1986 team.

Boog Powell Takes Advantage of an Oriole Perk—At Least Two Cases of National

The happy interplay between the local brewery and the local ball club was appreciated by Boog Powell. The Orioles' all-star first baseman recalled that during his tenure with the Birds in the late 1960s and early '70s, every Oriole got two free cases of National beer at the beginning of every home stand.

A Satisfying History of Charm City Brewing

Boog Powell in the *Miller Lite Celebrity Guide*, 1987. *Courtesy Miller Lite.*

Boog later achieved national notoriety as one of the jovial gang of former athletes appearing in Miller Lite television advertisements. Powell recalled that as an Oriole, he was quick to relieve the few teetotalers on the club of their complimentary cases of the owner's beer. "Sometimes you could collect eight to ten cases per home stand," Powell said.

"I liked Natty Boh," Powell said, using the nickname of National Bohemian beer. As he stretched out in his home, Powell recalled that after games, he and teammates Terry Crowley, Curt Blefary and Brooks Robinson would often tap some of their free beer when they gathered in the backyards of their row homes on Medford Road a few blocks away from Memorial Stadium for late-night crab feasts. "I was loyal to National," Powell said. "If you lived in Baltimore, by God you drank the Baltimore beer."

From Scoreboards to the Bay: Battles for Beer Advertisements

Wherever sportsmen gathered, from the ballpark to the Chesapeake Bay to the bowling alley, Baltimore breweries battled for their patronage.

Ballpark scoreboards, for instance, were prime spots for beer advertisements and therefore were hotly contested turf. A Gunther ad dominated the scoreboard

Gunther battled National for Oriole fans, as this 1954 scorecard adorned with a Gunther ad shows. *Courtesy David Hoffberger.*

at the old Oriole Park, at Twenty-ninth and Greenmount, that burned down in 1944. Gunther also had advertising on the center field scoreboard for the first year, 1954, that the Orioles played at Memorial Stadium on Thirty-third Street. Zanvyl Krieger sat on the Oriole board of directors, and so for the first year, his family's beer, Gunther, was on the board. Hoffberger's beer, National, did not get the scoreboard spot until 1970.

The scoreboard at Bugle Field, the Edison Highway home of Baltimore's Elite (pronounced "ee-light") Giants of the Negro baseball league, was sponsored by Arrow beer. Trabert, a Baltimore native, fondly recalled going with his father to Giants games as young man. "The baseball was very good," Trabert said, "and the home plate umpire was a comedian. He would talk back and forth with the fans. He would go into the stands. It was some fun."

A Satisfying History of Charm City Brewing

An Arrow beer advertisement, circa 1950s, aimed at Maryland hunters. *Courtesy David Donovan Collection. Photo by Edward Brown.*

Boaters on the Chesapeake Bay were also targeted by breweries. National dispatched radio personality "Commodore" Frank Hennessey, an affable Irishman who worked at National from 1957 to 1975, to wheel a skipjack christened the *Chester Peake* around the bay, passing out National beer in eight-ounce cans called "skippers." American Brewery ran its own Chesapeake Bay promotion, promising a whopping amount of cash to the fisherman who landed "Diamond Jim III," a rockfish tagged with a diamond-shaped marker.

Baltimore breweries also sponsored horse races at local tracks, boxing matches and wrestling matches. A televised bowling program, *Bowling for Dollars*, sponsored by National and presided over by the exuberant Bailey Goss, became a fixture in Baltimore popular culture. Goss, who died at age forty-nine in 1962 after a traffic accident at Falls Road and Cold Spring Lane, was a charming man and a close friend and colleague of Chuck Thompson, who spoke fondly of him in the March 2005 interview.

"Bailey was a terrific-looking man," Thompson recalled. "He captured women's attention and men's admiration. He would make an appearance, looking great in a blue shirt, and the next day guys would be downtown asking the clerks in the Eddie Jacobs shop [in downtown Baltimore] for the shirt Bailey Goss wore the night before. Bailey was probably more responsible than anyone else for the success of National Brewing Company. And he looked like guy who enjoyed a beer. Many people said when Bailey talked about National Beer it was difficult to stay away from the refrigerator."

Goss also was the guy who poured the beer during live TV commercials between innings of Orioles games. Sometimes, however, the duty fell to Thompson, and that, he recalled, "drove me crazy." The head of the beer needed to look just right—"full and frothy without overflowing," Thompson said. "It couldn't fall short of the top of the glass, and it couldn't spill over. I quickly learned that salt made the beer foam. Let me tell you, the Orioles could have pulled out a win in extra innings, but if the head on the beer didn't look right, it was a long day at the ballpark. Thank the Lord for salt!"

Another local fellow, *Evening Sun* newspaper reporter turned television announcer Jim McManus, started his storied career as the host of *The National Sports Parade*, sponsored by National Bohemian Beer, and gave the latest results from local horse racing tracks.

It was Baltimore's first hit TV show on WMAR Channel 2, five afternoons per week from 3:00 p.m. to 5:00 p.m. The young McManus went on to New York, where at the suggestion of a network executive he changed his name to Jim McKay. He later became the anchor of *ABC's Wide World of Sports*, covering twelve Olympics. His marathon work at the 1972 games in Munich, when masked Palestinian terrorists took Israeli athletes hostage in their Olympic dormitory, resulting in the deaths of eleven athletes, won him worldwide acclaim and set a new standard for excellence in television sports journalism. When Jim McKay made his 1947 television debut—a report of two horse races—it was panned in print by none other than H.L. Mencken, who said that the young man doing commentary was not very good. But decades later, after McKay died at his Monkton farm in 2008, he was hailed around America as the model for the modern sports anchorman.

Beer and Food

Long before there were the craft beer dinners of today, venerable Baltimore beer makers were exploring the gustatory pleasures of beer.

For instance, in the 1940s, the president of the National Brewing Company, Arthur H. Deute, was a gourmet of a national renown. He founded a fine dining group, Les Amis D'Escoffier, that at its peak had seventeen thousand members throughout America. He wrote a weekly cooking column for the Bell newspaper syndicate, and a collection of his recipes were published as a book in 1944 under the title *200 Dishes for Men to Cook*. One of his noteworthy efforts was creating a dish called four and twenty blackbirds baked in a pie. Deute substituted squab, but the dish, served at a gathering at the Belvedere Hotel, garnered headlines around the country. The birds were served with wine, Pinot Noir, but Deute caused some commotion in gastronomic circles when he repeatedly said that beer—no doubt he was thinking of his brewery's National Premium—was a better partner with some meat dishes than wine.

When the privations brought on by the efforts to supply the troops during World War II caused shortages, Deute's fine dining group also scaled back. "Quel Horreur!" proclaimed a headline in the March 19, 1942 edition of the *Sun*, "Les Amis Will Eat Ordinary Food." Among the "ordinary" fare was beer.

On a less lofty front, Baltimore breweries regularly urged kitchen cooks to use beer as an ingredient in home-cooked meals. The major breweries issued free publications, some elaborate, some not, but all containing recipes that called for beer.

Beer and crabs, a pairing pushed by many Baltimore breweries, including National Bohemian. *Photo by Jim Burger.*

In 1948, for example, during the start of its decade-long run as the city's dominant beer, the National Brewing Company published a thirty-four-page booklet called *Brew in Your Stew*. The booklet was adorned with illustrations of a beer-drinking, bow tie–wearing gentleman, a Ward Cleaver in an apron, stirring up beery delights. It was a marketing ploy aimed at coaxing men into the kitchen, where they presumably would pour National Premium into soups and stews, not just into themselves.

The Gunther Hostess and the "Grin Game"

Another landmark 1950s Baltimore beer maker, Gunther Brewing Company, took a slightly different approach to promoting the notion of getting more beer in more kitchens. It published *The Gunther Hostess Book*, in which an unnamed but attractive pearl-wearing hostess offered advice on "the joys of gracious living." This post–World War II hostess—a Martha Stewart with a Gunther six-pack in her pantry—promised readers "clever games to play at your parties," among them the grin game, in which "the boys are to grin as broadly as possible, with a tape measure deciding the winner." In addition, she offered pages of recipes, some using "Gunther's Dry Beer-Y Beer, the dry, tangy beer that never kills your appetite and adds to the joy of gracious living."

A Satisfying History of Charm City Brewing

Not to be outdone, Globe Brewery, makers of Arrow beer, included "12 Unusual Tested Recipes with Arrow Beer" in the brochure that explained its brewing process to the beer-drinking public. Among the dishes described in it were a Welsh rarebit—basically a melted hot cheese sandwich—and a mixture of hot beer, cinnamon and lemon peel touted as a "a good drink for a cold night," plus the Chesapeake Bay classic, hard crabs steamed with beer.

BEER AND FOOD, A TRICKY COUPLING

Today, craft brewers not only embrace the idea that beer has a spot at the dinner table, but they have also taken it several steps further. They get down to specifics, advising beer drinkers into two areas: how to match styles of beer with various dishes and how to use different types of craft beer as ingredients in dishes.

One widely suggested tactic in the matching game is finding the common flavor and aroma elements that the beer and the food share. For example, the nutty flavor of an English-style ale goes well with a handmade cheddar cheese, the deep roasted flavors of an imperial stout pairs well with chocolate truffles and the rich caramel flavors of an Oktoberfest lager are recommended when eating roast pork.

Another approach is to consider the weight or flavor profiles of the eats and drinks. In this scheme, lighter lagers and ales are happier with soups, fondues or chicken dishes, while darker, more robust beers are drawn to red meats.

Even the chemistry of hops and malts and how they perform on the tongue have been given once-overs. The sweetness of malt reduces the heat of spicy foods, according to Julia Herz, a certified beer judge with the Association of Craft Brewers, the national craft beer association based in Boulder, Colorado. Since sweet kills heat, Herz advises drinking a malty brown ale to tame spicy Thai dishes or a Scotch ale to quell fiery Mexican fare.

As for hops, their bitterness cuts through fat of sauces, and that helps the palate sense more of the flavors in a dense dish. A good rule of thumb, Herz advises, is to pick a hoppy beer to go with rich or fatty fare and a malty brew for spicy dishes.

The burgeoning business of matching beer and food has not escaped the notice of mainstream brewers. In 2007, Anheuser-Busch, working with *Sunset* magazine put out the *Great Food Great Beer* cookbook, with 185 recipes pairing beer with food. Among the tips it offered were that goat cheese goes well with wheat beer and that roast asparagus with lemon matches up well with pale ale. The massive St. Louis brewery, now owned by the global brewer In-Bev, so far has not changed its time-honored slogan to "This Bud matches well with spicy pork ribs," but who knows what the future holds.

On the cooking front, more amateurs and professional chefs are using beer as an ingredient. It can be tricky. Authors of the lively *Dog Chow Cook Book, Volume I*, put out by Flying Dog Brewery, issue a blunt warning: "Don't boil beer, especially hoppy beers such as pale ales or IPAs." Boiling beer increases the bitterness of hops, and that, the Flying Dog cooking crew reports, is not a good thing. If you boil fish in beer at high heat rather than poaching it in beer at low heat, your fish, they warn, will "end up tasting like a hop farm."

Marylanders have a tradition of steaming shellfish over beer, but as John Shields, the Baltimore restaurateur and author of Chesapeake Bay cookbooks, has noted, the locals use flat beer for cooking shellfish. Flat beer, which has lost its carbonation, does not produce the harsh, metallic flavors when it is boiled that fresh beer does. "Flat beer is milder," said Shields, who grew up in a Baltimore household where steaming shellfish was a ritual.

Most of the steaming recipes in the vintage Gunther, National and Arrow recipe books call for flat beer. Beer goes flat if left in a bowl at room

Linking fine dining and beer, breweries provided to Baltimore restaurants menu covers like this one from Gunther. *Courtesy David Hoffberger.*

temperature for an hour or two; alternatively, Shields said, you can hasten the process by sprinkling salt into the bowl of brew.

The question of whether beery steam can actually penetrate the hard shells of the crabs is open to debate, Shields acknowledged. But he was adamant that the aroma of crabs steaming over flat beer was a major part of the culinary endeavor. "I have steamed crabs without beer, just using vinegar," Shields said. "It didn't smell right. It wasn't the same experience."

The reason flat beer is milder is because it has lost the sharp mineral bite that comes with carbonation, said Herz, of the National Craft Brewers Association. Putting salt in a beer breaks the carbon dioxide out of the solution, she said, and without carbon dioxide, the beer goes flat.

Marinating, or giving meats and chicken a beer bath before cooking them, is another tactic. The beer adds flavor, and its moderate acidity weakens muscles tissue, which helps to retain moisture, meaning it is harder for a cook to turn a piece of marinated meat into leather.

Behaving like true Marylanders, National beer executives roll up their sleeves to eat crabs and drink beer. *Courtesy David Hoffberger.*

The hot barbecue grill and the cold beer have been longtime if casual companions. But their relationship has become more celebrated. Steven Raichlen, an internationally known barbecue guru and a native of Baltimore, filled his 2002 *Beer-Can Chicken* book with seventy-five recipes marrying the two. Essentially, the beer can cooking method calls for massaging a chicken with spicy rub and then inserting an open half-full can of beer—either twelve-ounce or sixteen-ounce—between its legs. Using the chicken legs and the beer can as a tripod, the bird is placed upright on the grill and then cooked near, but not over, the fire for an hour or two with the cooker lid closed. The beer adds moisture and some flavor to the bird. The beer, however, is shot.

Baking and beer have a storied history together. As Harold McGee pointed out in his seminal 1984 work *On Food and Cooking*, the ancient Egyptians used beer froth, the sediment of the fermenting brew, to leaven their bread. By the nineteenth century, the preferred method of baking bread in England was using beer froth as a leavening ingredient. It produces the "finest, lightest bread," wrote A. Edlin in his 1805 *Treatise on the Art of Breadmaking*. That union is still popular today, as sources ranging from *The Joy of Cooking* to the Food Network have recipes that yield loaves of bread by mixing flour, salt, sugar and beer.

Kitchen Experiments with Beer

Mixing the old and the new, I tried vintage and modern recipes that used beer as an ingredient.

First bowing to Baltimore's beery past, I tried several of the retro recipes detailed in the Gunther, Arrow and National publications. Some worked well. Some didn't. Some were a hoot.

One evening, for example, following the advice of the Gunther Hostess, I started the meal with a so-called Baltimore Salad, a Jell-O-like concoction made with beer and unflavored gelatin. Making such a salad, the Gunther Hostess advised, gave "the homemaker an opportunity to display her inventive genius."

Apparently, the Gunther Hostess had more genius in the beer-as-salad field than I was able to muster. She, it seemed, was able to master the central tenet of this creation, namely making beer stand still. I tried following the recipe for Baltimore Salad set down in the Gunther booklet. I mixed plain gelatin with boiling water, salt, sugar, lemon juice and a bottle of beer. Since

Fred Bauernschmidt's American Brewery at Hillen and Monument Streets was Baltimore's largest pre-prohibition brewery, producing some 400,000 barrels per year. *Photo Jim Burger.*

National animated characters. *Photo by Jim Burger.*

"Matchless Body," one of the Arrow pinup girls whose ranks may have included Marilyn Monroe. *Courtesy David Donovan.*

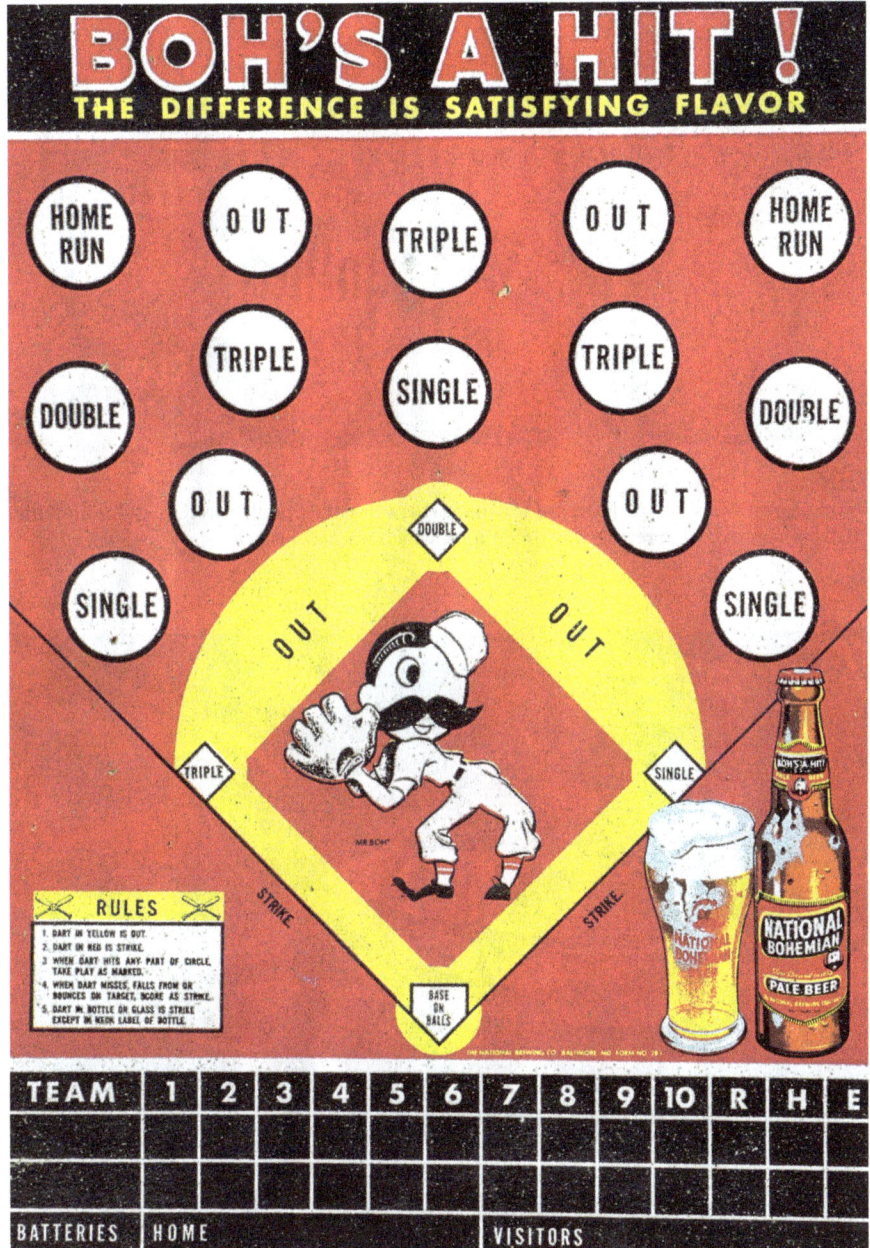

In the late 1950s and into the 1960s, Baltimore saloons were decorated with dartboards like this one, from National Bohemian, simulating a baseball game. *Photo by Jim Burger.*

Beer cans with cone-shaped tops, which made them resemble bottles, were popular until the 1950s, when they were replaced with flat tops, which stacked easily. *Photo by Jim Burger.*

Gunther advertisement, circa 1950, promoting peace, a brighter tomorrow and traveling by helicopter. *Photo by Edward Brown.*

Right: Baltimore's big breweries—Arrow, Gunther and National—promoted the idea of serving beer with fine food. *Photo by Jim Burger.*

Below: A temple of malt and hops, the former Wiessner and American brewery has been restored to its former glory. *Courtesy the Baltimore Sun.*

Left: Hugh Sisson opened Sisson's, the state's first brewpub, in 1989 and went on to found Clipper City Brewing Company, brewer of Heavy Seas beers. *Photo by Jim Burger.*

Below: Painting in Baltimore's Flag House showing Mary Pickersgill, working in a brewery and sewing the flag that would fly over Fort McHenry and inspire the creation of the national anthem. *Photo by Jim Burger.*

Right: Renovated National beer plant is now a mix of offices and is filling up with new generations of beer drinkers. *Photo by Alexander D. Mitchell IV.*

Below: Brewmaster Matt Brophy stands in front of the Flying Dog Brewery, which moved to Maryland from Colorado in 2006. *Courtesy Flying Dog.*

Poster advertising Fred Bauernschmidt's brewery, the state's largest before prohibition. *Courtesy David Donovan Collection. Photo by Edward Brown.*

Placard for Darley Park brewery and beer garden at the end of the Harford Road streetcar line, a favorite spot of H.L. Mencken. *Courtesy David Donovan Collection. Photo by Edward Brown.*

Once the Orioles arrived in Baltimore in 1954, scoreboards tracking the team's inning-by-inning tallies were common in the city's taverns. *Courtesy David Donovan Collection. Photo by Edward Brown.*

Above: Gunther's version of the tavern baseball scoreboard. *Courtesy David Donovan Collection. Photo by Edward Brown.*

Opposite, top: A light advertising Arrow Beer, brewed for a time by the GBS beer trust. *Courtesy David Donovan Collection. Photo by Edward Brown.*

Opposite, bottom: An outdoor light advertising Gunther's beer. *Courtesy David Donovan Collection. Photo by Edward Brown.*

Above: Separate tavern entrances for ladies could be found in Baltimore well into the 1970s. *Courtesy David Donovan Collection. Photo by Edward Brown.*

Right: A cold beer is a good beer, as this polar bear poster made in Baltimore proclaims. *Courtesy Library of Congress.*

Opposite, top: An outdoor light advertising Free State, a beer that was born after prohibition. *Courtesy David Donovan Collection. Photo by Edward Brown.*

Opposite, bottom: Mr. Boh, the mascot representing National Bohemian beer, on a globe light. *Courtesy David Donovan Collection. Photo by Edward Brown.*

In a pitch to Baltimore's factory workers, Mr. Boh carries a lunch pail. *Courtesy David Hoffberger.*

Former Oriole slugger John "Boog" Powell celebrates after tapping a cask that opened the first Baltimore Beer Week in October 2009 as members of Beer Week committee cheer him on. *Photo by Alexander D. Mitchell IV.*

Brian Strumke, a self-described gypsy brewer based in Baltimore, makes Stillwater Artisanal Ales. *Photo by Charles D. Cook.*

Brewer's Art owners Tom Creegan, hoisting a beer, and Volker Stewart. *Photo by Jim Burger.*

Left: Staffer Jose Antonio happily hoists mugs of Pub Dog beers in its tavern in Federal Hill. *Photo by Jim Burger.*

Below: Pratt Street Ale House brewmaster Stephen Jones rests his arms on taps of Oliver beers, one of many ales brewed at its downtown location. *Photo by Jim Burger.*

A Satisfying History of Charm City Brewing

Gunther's hasn't been available for over half a century, I used another local lager, a pilsner.

I poured this mixture into a metal mold shaped in a circle and put the mold in the bottom of fridge. The salad refused to congeal. It sloshed around in an unruly way. It took a full day of chilling on the bottom shelf of the refrigerator before the salad began to resemble the well-behaved gelatin mold the Gunther Hostess had described. When I sliced it and served it with some sour cream, this Baltimore Salad quickly melted into a disappointing puddle of pilsner.

On another aromatic night, I did what the title of the National cooking booklet advised. I put a brew in my stew. I poured a cup of pale lager onto a thick, round steak and then let the meat cook with vegetables and rice in covered pot for a few hours in a 350-degree oven. The steak emerged from its beer bath tender but somewhat bland. The rice, however, was wonderful.

The beer-soaked ham seemed to be a favorite of old Baltimore. I made one, using the recipe, called Easter Ham, Polish style, from the National booklet. It called for making a paste of brown sugar, beer, mustard and cinnamon and then coating a precooked, clove-studded ham with the paste and baking it for about an hour in a 350-degree oven. Despite the fact that my paste was thin, the result of pouring too much beer in the mixture, the dish was pleasing.

The exterior of the ham developed a crisp, sweet crust. None of the tasters seemed sure what effect, if any, the beer had on the flavor of the ham. Whether the ham was flavorful because it had been pasted with beer or with brown sugar didn't seem to matter. What mattered was the result: a good hunk of ham for supper.

For a vintage dessert, I made a beer cake. I got the recipe from the Gunther Hostess. It called for bananas, cinnamon, sugar and flour. I substituted DuClaw porter, a local brew, for the "a half cup of Gunther's Beery Beer" that she recommended.

The cake, a big brown sheet cake, turned out to be a triumph. It had a sweet, banana-bread flavor. There were mixed reviews of the lemon icing that accompanied the cake. Some thought the icing was better than the cake. Others disdained the icing and feasted on the sheet cake, even eating a few slices the next morning, an action that puts them in the dubious company of characters who enjoy beer at breakfast.

Next, using recipes pulled from current sources—cookbooks, websites and brewery publications—I made a variety of dishes with beer. It was a bumpy road. I brined chicken wings for eight hours in a solution brimming with salt, spices, fruit juice and India Pale Ale. When I grilled these wings, they were plump and flavorful but overall not worth the eight hours of waiting. I bathed a steak in marinade made of stout, Worcestershire and Tabasco sauces, but it ended up tasting more of Worcestershire than beer. I made brownies with a smidgen of coffee stout. They were dry and disappointing.

I had better luck when we popped the top on simpler fare: bread, brats and a couple of soups. Bread making has a primal feel to it, and the beer bread I made by mixing several cups of flour, a little sugar, some rolled oats and bottle of ale was elementary and delicious.

Braising bratwurst in butter, onions and beer probably goes back to the early days of Germany, and it is one custom I am glad made it across the Atlantic Ocean. First the sausages took a dip in a skillet filled with the beer mixture, then I tossed them over a charcoal grill fire. Next I cooked down the beer, butter and onions in the skillet to make a delectable relish.

There are many theories in Maryland about what kind of beer to serve with crabs. It depends on the crabs, Hugh Sisson of Clipper City Brewing told a seminar in June 2008 on Chesapeake Bay seafood as part of a Savor, a three-day event in Washington, D.C., that paired craft beers with food. The event, organized by the Craft Brewers Association, drew forty-eight craft brewers from around the nation and a crowd of 2,100.

For steamed crabs that are covered with peppery spices, you need a beer with good malt content and a mild amount of hops, Sisson said. If the beer is too bitter, it will overpower the crabmeat, and if the bitterness of the hops is too high, the bitterness of the peppers will dominate, he said. The beers in his Heavy Seas lineup that matched this profile would be pales and pilsners, Sisson said. Crab cakes, flavored with mustard and Old Bay seasoning, would match up well with marzen-style lagers, which also work with soft crabs, he said.

Meanwhile, the new brewers in Maryland (or "come-heres" in the local parlance), Flying Dog, have come up with what they say is a perfect partner for a crab chowder: a wheat beer. For some time, the workers at the Frederick brewery had been sharing beer-based recipes, and in 2010, they compiled them in volume one of the *Dog Chow Cookbook*, a small publication now out of print. In it was a recipe from brewer Vince Chase, a former chef, who used the brewery's In-Heat Wheat Hefeweizen in a fiery crab chowder. The beer's banana and clove flavors would complement the spice of the Old Bay, Chase said. I was doubtful, but after making this chowder, we all had to agree with the new arrivals from Colorado.

A Satisfying History of Charm City Brewing

Sometimes newcomers bring fresh ideas to old traditions. This is one. It was, however, topped in the beer-soup category by a sweet potato, apple and beer mixture created by cookbook author Crescent Dragonwagon. Her beer soup is the best ever.

Here are some old and a few new recipes using beer as an ingredient.

Dishes of a Bygone Era

Hard Crabs Steamed with Arrow Beer

1 dozen hard crabs
1 cup vinegar
1 teaspoon salt
½ teaspoon pepper
1 heaping teaspoon dry mustard
2 12-ounce bottles of Arrow beer (substitute flat lager or ale)

Place crabs in pot with false bottom or place tin pie plate in bottom of pot to keep the crabs out of the liquid. Sprinkle dry ingredients (salt, pepper and mustard) over the crabs and then pour the beer and vinegar over the crabs. Steam in a tightly closed pot for 20 to 25 minutes or until crabs are uniformly red.

Old-Fashioned Rarebit

1 pound American (cheddar) cheese, shredded
1 tablespoon butter
2 tablespoons salt
2 tablespoons dry mustard
1 teaspoon paprika
6 ounces Arrow (lager) beer

Using a heavy saucepan or a very clean frying pan, melt the butter and, under low fire, stir in the salt, pepper, paprika and mustard. Add the shredded cheese and stir until melted. Then add the beer slowly, stirring continuously until very smooth. Pour at once over toast and serve on a heated dish.

Baltimore Beer

Gunther's Spice Cake

1⅓ cups sugar
⅓ cup soft butter
3 egg yolks, beaten
½ cup Gunther's Dry Beery Beer (substitute a lager)
1 teaspoon baking soda
1 cup banana pulp (about 2 large ripe bananas, mashed into pulp)
1 teaspoon salt
2 teaspoons cinnamon
3 cups sifted flour
3 teaspoons baking powder

Preheat oven to 350 degrees. In a mixer, cream sugar and butter, and add the beaten egg yolks. In a separate bowl, blend flour, baking powder, cinnamon, baking soda and salt. With mixer on low, gradually add portions of the dry ingredients to the butter, egg and sugar mixture and then add portions of the beer. Repeat until dry ingredients and beer are used up. When this mixture is well blended, gradually add the banana pulp and blend. Put batter in an 8½- by 11-inch loaf pan that has been greased with butter. Bake until toothpick inserted in the middle of the cake can be inserted and removed without signs of batter, about 30 to 35 minutes. Cover with a lemon frosting.

New Era Eating

Flying Dog Crab Chowder

4 green onions, chopped
3 celery stalks, chopped
2 teaspoons garlic, minced
2 tablespoons bacon drippings
½ cup Flying Dog in Heat Hefeweizen, or other wheat beer
1 cup chicken stock
2 ears fresh corn, kernels removed from cob
½ pound crabmeat
½–1 tablespoon Old Bay seasoning
¼ teaspoon red pepper flakes

1 tablespoon fresh parsley, chopped
1 bay leaf
1½ cups milk, room temperature
4 tablespoons butter
4 tablespoons flour

In a large saucepan, cook sufficient amount of bacon strips (4 good sized) to yield 2 tablespoons of bacon drippings. When cooked, remove bacon strips from pan. Add chopped onions, celery and garlic to pan and sauté until they soften, about 5 minutes. Add the beer, chicken stock, kernels of corn, milk and all the spices. Gently bring to low boil and then simmer until the corn is cooked, about 7 minutes. Add crabmeat, folding into mixture; turn heat to low and cover pan. In a small separate pan, melt the butter. Then, with pan over low heat, gradually add 4 tablespoons of flour, whisking vigorously and continuously. Continue whisking for several minutes until flour is absorbed and the mixture turns a dark, nutty brown. When mixture has thickened, stir it into the crab and corn mixture. Warm to desired serving temperature. This chowder is spicy. Serve with beer bread. Adapted from the *Dog Chow Cookbook, Volume I*.

BEER BREAD
Yield: 1 loaf

1 cup whole wheat flour
1 cup white flour
½ cup rolled oats
2 tablespoons baking soda
½ teaspoon baking powder
½ teaspoon salt
12 ounces of beer, lager or ale

Rub the interior of a 9- by 5-inch loaf pan with butter. Preheat oven to 400 degrees. In a large bowl, combine all the dry ingredients. Gradually add the beer and mix well. Mixture should be moist. Spread it evenly in loaf pan. Bake until a probe inserted in the middle of the loaf all the way to the bottom emerges without any mixture on it, about 35 minutes. Remove from loaf pan and let cool on a wire rack for 5 to 10 minutes before slicing.

Baltimore Beer

Beer and Sweet Potato Soup

¼ cup dark raisins
1 bottle pilsner, 12 ounces
4 tablespoons butter
1 onion, diced
2 tart apples, unpeeled, cored and diced
1 tablespoon curry powder
2 teaspoons finely minced ginger root
2 tablespoons flour
4 cups chicken or vegetable stock
½ cup thawed frozen apple juice
1 piece of cinnamon stick, about 1 inch long
1 teaspoon soy sauce
2 medium sweet potatoes, peeled and finely diced
salt and pepper to taste

In a bowl, soak the raisins in the beer for at least half an hour, or overnight if possible. Melt the butter in a 10-inch skillet over medium heat. Add the onion and sauté until it softens, about three minutes. Add the diced apples and sauté again until the apples are somewhat soft, about 4 minutes. Sprinkle with curry powder, turning down the heat to low and stirring often, for about eight minutes. Stir in the ginger and cook for two more minutes. Drain the raisins, saving both the beer and the raisins. Sprinkle the flour over the apple mixture and cook over low heat for about a minute. Gradually add the beer, stirring to smooth any lumps, and cook until hot, smooth and free of flour taste, about six minutes. Put this mixture in a food processor, add the raisins and process until smooth.

In a heavy soup pot, combine the stock (vegetable or chicken), the apple juice concentrate, the cinnamon stick and the soy sauce. Bring to boil, add the sweet potatoes and turn down the heat. Simmer, partially covered, until the potatoes are tender, about 30 minutes.

Remove the cinnamon stick from the hot stock and stir in the apple puree. Season with salt and white pepper. Add more apple juice to taste, more soy sauce or a pinch of cayenne pepper to add spice. Simmer over low heat for several minutes more to meld the flavors. Serve with dollops of sour cream, crème fraîche or yogurt. Adapted from "Dairy Hollow Soup and Bread" by Crescent Dragonwagon.

Collectors

They mine the city's sudsy past. They are collectors of Baltimore's breweriana, the stuff of the city's beery history. They are students of the artwork, posters, lamps, openers, coasters, tip jars, bottles and cans of years ago—the flotsam and jetsam of the great river of local beers that once flowed through Baltimore, their town.

They come from various lines of work. When they get together, what they talk about is not what they did today but rather what they saved from yesteryear. Here two collectors of Baltimore breweriana explain why they enjoy rooting through pieces of the past. In the process, they give history lessons.

Joe Trabert

Joseph C. Trabert Jr., a native of west Baltimore, has taught elementary school, served as Baltimore city film commissioner and has been an environmental specialist for the Maryland Department of Transportation. He also makes a mean hot sauce from the peppers that he and his wife, Sherry, grow in the front yard of their Hamilton neighborhood home.

But he is best known as the former proprietor of a Fells Point bar called Turkey Joe's. The bar, at 710 South Broadway, became a meeting place from 1972 to 1980 for a crowd of fun seekers, cops and media types, including a group dubbed "the Fellowship of Christian Journalists." Occasionally, the regulars of Turkey Joe's meet for a reunion at the old bar, which is now Alexander's Tavern.

The back of the bar of Turkey Joe's featured an immense collection of beer cans. How that collection got started is one of the intriguing tales that Turkey Joe recounts.

Joe Trabert, who once filled his Fells Point bar, Turkey Joe's, with beer cans, holds a Pabst can in front of the tower on South Charles and Wells Streets that was used as a bottling facility by Pabst and closed when prohibition hit. *Photo by Jim Burger.*

When I opened the bar, a beer drummer, a salesman, came in one day and gave me some mint Gunther and National display cans—air cans, sealed at the bottom and the top, brand new, gorgeous shape.

I put them up on the bar. So a guy, Charlie Miller, the oldest collector in Baltimore, came in one night and said, "I would like to have those, and I will give you a hundred beer cans for two of them." I said you have a deal. He left right then, went back to his house off Harford Road and brought me one hundred different beer cans, and that was the basis of my collection.

Then I put a sign up—"Gimme a beer can I don't have and I will give you a draft." That is what I did.

A Satisfying History of Charm City Brewing

Then we had a guy, Joe, who was a distributor for out-of-town beers. He would bring a case of these beers, we called them mystery beers. We would sell them for fifty cents, about half of what other beers sold for. The "mystery beer" would be poured in a glass, and the can would go up into the collection.

I sold the bar in 1980 when I got married. There are the three "Ws" associated with running a bar: whiskey, women and weakness. I have got a good marriage and don't regret selling the bar.

I have since sold some of my beer can collection, the stuff that isn't from Baltimore. But I once collected anything from a church key (a can or bottle opener) to a growler (a jug used to carry draft beer). I collected wooden beer cases, paper labels, crowns or bottle caps.

Some people collect only beer stuff that is pre- or post-prohibition, but not me. I collected on both sides of the Eighteenth Amendment. Collectors who do not have access to old, expensive stuff save coasters, bottles, tap handles and other products from current-day brewpubs and small breweries. As I traveled around Baltimore's watering holes, I confess that I gathered a few of these current-day collectibles. You never knew when something might become valuable.

I also collected the mainstay of breweriana, beer cans. I have cans from Baltimore's best-known breweries—National, Gunther, American, Arrow, Free State. I have them in a variety of styles and fashions—the steel beer cans of Pittsburgh's Iron City, the cone-shaped cans of National, even camouflage cans used during World War II.

Although there is some dispute about exactly when beer was first put in a can, there is general agreement that the can of Krueger beer that came out of that Newark, New Jersey brewery on January 23, 1935, is among the earliest, if not the first, of the species.

National beer cone-top cans on parade. *Photo by Jim Burger.*

Krueger, and later other brewers, chose Richmond, Virginia, as the nation's first test market for beer in cans.

Richmond is not very far away from Baltimore, at least in the view of collectors like me. Beer can collectors have an interesting way of hunting for our treasured old cans. They look for spots near taverns or old gas stations—in the South, gas stations sold beer—that once were repositories, or "dumps," for old cans. Back in the days before recycling, beer drinkers simply tossed their cans into the countryside. These dumps have proved to be treasure-troves for beginning collectors. I have found old, rare cans, in good shape, surrounded by rusting beer and soda cans.

Virginia is an especially rich area for old beer cans. In other words, it is a good place to "go dumping." In addition to the hope that you might find a Krueger can, there is also a chance you might find some rare National Bohemian cans. National Bohemian tried out a lot of their new containers, including aluminum cans, in Virginia.

Like a lot of beer can collectors, my interest in the field blossomed when I was in college. I graduated from the University of Maryland in the 1950s, when College Park was little more than a cow town. I used to go to the Varsity bar and buy a "pound of beer," sixteen ounces for fifty cents. As a young man, I began putting cans on a ledge. This method served both as a way of collecting beer cans and keeping track of how much beer you were drinking.

The guys I ran around with when we went "down the ocean" to Ocean City used to make "beeramids," structures similar to the Egyptian pyramids, except these were made out of beer cans. Woe be unto the lad who, while attempting to place his freshly emptied can of National Bohemian or Esslinger (a beer brewed in Philadelphia) on the top of the structure, ended up knocking down the beeramid.

I also collected beer glasses. Glasses come in different sizes. Pilsner glasses, for instance, are long, cylindrical glasses that allow the bubbles in the pilsner style of beer to gracefully ascend to the top of the glass. In my view, it is a good idea every so often to stop and watch the pilsner bubbles rise.

One reason I collected beer glasses is that they are utilitarian. You can drink your favorite brew out of them. You can display them. Usually they are not expensive. That is because a majority of beer glass collections owe their beginnings to theft. The scenario usually goes something like this. A drinker, it might be me, it might be another upstanding citizen, is sitting in a bar sucking down a Boh when it dawns on him that this glass would sure look good in his place. I could drink out of it, and show it off, he thinks to himself. He pockets the glass. The next bar he visits has a different beer name emblazoned on the glass. He puts this glass in his sock and pulls his pant leg over it. And so we have it, a hobby with its roots in theft.

Nowadays, modern microbrewers sell their pint-size and twenty-ounce glasses. This practice serves as an advertisement for the brewery, it cuts down on theft and it prevents those unsightly beer glass bulges from forming at your ankle under your pant leg.

MIKE BOWLER

Mike Bowler is a native of Helena, Montana, and graduated from high school there in 1959. He went to college in New York City, getting an undergraduate and a master's degree from Columbia University. He embarked on a career in journalism, working at a variety of newspapers before landing in Baltimore in 1970. At the Evening Sun, *he wrote editorials and edited the paper's op-edit page. When the* Evening Sun *folded, he moved to the morning paper, the* Baltimore Sun, *where he covered education, kindergarten to college. After writing for close to thirty-five years at the Baltimore newspapers, he went to work in 2004 for the U.S. Department of Education in Washington and retired from full-time work in 2007. He offers this synopsis of his collecting history.*

I started collecting beer cans in the late 1970s. Thirty-some years later, I'm still collecting, though the hobby for me has evolved from quantity to quality, and I've long since branched out to collecting "breweriana"—trays, bottle caps, matchbooks, ash trays, coasters and the like. Still, the beer can is the heart of my collection. There is nothing like opening a cold one and repairing to the basement, where my two thousand or so cans are displayed along two walls in alphabetical order. Then I caress a few of my favorites. No offense, but you really can't do that satisfactorily with a stamp collection.

Beer can collecting is a distinctly male-oriented and more-than-a-little-chauvinistic hobby, and I'm not embarrassed by that. Beer, after all, has always been marketed primarily to men. Try to imagine two women engaging in that classic Miller Lite debate, "Tastes Great, Less Filling," or dispatching a dog from the poker room to fetch a couple of Strohs. It is a fact that until only a few years ago, the annual "canvention" of the Beer Can Collectors of America (now the Brewery Collectibles Club of America) featured a Miss Beer Can.

Another thing those cans do for me is bring back memories, large and small, from my seventy years on the planet. Miss Rheingold takes me back to my salad days in New York City. A Kessler Beer cone top from Helena, Montana, conjures my dad sipping a Kessler while driving home from the state fair—I think he had had a few at the fair. The labels on a decade's worth of Iron City cans trace Pittsburgh's major sports heroes and championship teams of the '70s. And then there are cans and series of cans related to historical events, such as Falstaff's bicentennial series in 1976. My favorite in this category, though, is a can showing Mickey Mouse with an American flag in his right hand. The raised middle digit of Mickey's left hand points to this wording: "Hey, Iran! Protect Our Heritage. Free the hostages."

A New Breed of Baltimore Brewers

In 2012, Baltimore and its suburbs are awash in craft beers. Five craft breweries in Maryland are busy bottling locally made beers, and more such plants are on the drawing board. In addition, throughout the metropolitan area, more than a dozen brewpubs—restaurants where beer is brewed on the premises—are filling up with patrons who have a thirst for the complex, nuanced flavors of fresh, locally made beers. There also has been an expanding interest in growlers, the juglike vessels that are filled with draft beer. Efforts are underway to persuade Maryland lawmakers to permit growlers to be filled at bars, not just brewpubs.

The number of craft breweries and brewpubs has been growing in Maryland, yet the output of even the largest plant, Flying Dog in Frederick, could not compare to the size of the massive old breweries—National, Gunther, American, Bauernschmidt's and Wiessner—in the city's sudsy past. National and Gunther breweries, for instance, once each brewed more than 1 million barrels of beer per year. Flying Dog's capacity in 2011 was 115,000 barrels.

While the region's craft brewers are not as economically mighty as some of their predecessors, they are nonetheless growing in commercial clout and influence. Anyone trying to squeeze into the Brewer's Art brewpub in downtown Baltimore during Friday night happy hour, or into Red Brick Station in White Marsh on Tuesdays when brews go for one dollar a glass, knows all too well that craft brews draw crowds.

In addition, their ranks are swelling, as a surge of activity in 2012 showed. Jon Zerivitz plans to open Union Craft Brewing, an independent craft brewery in Clipper Mill, a former iron foundry and collection of buildings that in the 1800s was one of the largest manufacturing operations in America. Meanwhile, a two-hundred-seat beer-themed restaurant, Heavy Seas Ale House, debuted in the city's Little Italy neighborhood, and Stephen Demczuk, creator of the Raven beer, was eyeing an old bottling facility in the Waverly neighborhood as a potential home to a new operation called Charm City Brewery. In Harford County, DuClaw Brewing Company expanded its brewing operations, taking over a large building in Havre de Grace. In Frederick, the owners of Brewer's Alley converted an old ice cream plant to the Monocacy Brewing Company. On the Eastern Shore, Evolution Craft Brewing Company moved into a new, larger plant in Salisbury, and in Easton, entrepreneur Tim Miller was reviving an old Baltimore favorite, National Premium. In Columbia, Frisco and Tap Brew House announced plans to open a seven-barrel microbrewery under the name Push Cart Brewing.

This bubbling interest in local beer was not always the case. The current popularity comes after more than thirty years of trials, errors and successes by the new breed of Baltimore area brewers. These are their stories.

THE PIONEERS: BRITISH BREWING COMPANY AND SISSON'S

Baltimore's craft beer movement got started in a nondescript Glen Burnie industrial park. There, in 1988, two young transplants from Britain, Steve Parkes and Craig Stuart-Paul, had a fledgling operation called British Brewing Company. They had read market research reports saying that Bass ale, the hoppy beer that was a mainstay of England, sold well in taverns in the Baltimore-Washington area. The pair planned to make an English-style ale with its quick production time and mild flavor profile and produce it closer to the guys and gals who were drinking it. Beer, like bread, tastes better when it doesn't travel very far from its birthplace.

The Brits were surprised by Baltimore's hot summers. "One thing we didn't count on was the weather," said Parkes, who had a degree in brewing and seven years of experience working in British breweries. "It was so hot," Parkes told a reporter for the *Baltimore Sun* in 1989, "that the temperature went up in the fermenting process." In addition, the brewer also had trouble securing English hops and had to substitute American hops that "weren't right for the type of British brew we wanted to make."

Despite the drawbacks, the first kegs of Oxford Class, an ale with English malts and hops, rolled out of the Glen Burnie industrial park, a tract off

Ordnance Road chosen by the entrepreneurs for its central location, good water and low rent. Gradually, barrels of fresh beer found their way to taverns in Baltimore that served the locally made brew on draft. Unlike the historic attack on Fort McHenry, this British invasion was welcomed by the city.

In the cycle of beer brewing, the Baltimore area was experiencing an upswing. The large plants churning out beer for national distribution, like Hamm's, had folded, and the Carling-National Brewery on the beltway had suffered through a series of owners—G. Heileman and Stroh—before eventually closing in 1996. Yet smaller operations making premium beers for local markets popped up as fast as spring onions. In time, larger local breweries absorbed a few of the small upstarts on the scene, but others would emerge.

The Baltimore craft brewing movement born in Glen Burnie had begun with a roar. Thomas Cizauskas, a sharp observer of the local beer scene, wrote that the brewery's "old-fashioned propane gas-fired heating rings, submerged within the wort, would sound like a jet engine revving for take-off."

Over time, the British Brewing Company, a spirited pioneer, morphed into the Oxford Brewing Company in 1995, and for a while sales of its Raspberry Wheat beer helped its bottom line improve. But Raspberry Wheat alone could not keep the brewery going, and it closed in December 1998; Clipper City Brewing took over some of its brands.

Sisson's Clipper City Brewing: Heavy Seas Beers

The Baltimore brewing landscape took another notable and more permanent shift in the 1980s when Hugh Sisson decided to change careers. After working on a master's degree in theater at the University of Virginia, Sisson abandoned thoughts of becoming a professional actor and instead devoted himself to becoming a skilled brewer. In 1989, he opened a small brewing operation inside Sisson's, the south Baltimore bar that had been run by his father, Albert. The younger Sisson, working with Maryland state senator George Della, got the Maryland General Assembly to pass legislation allowing for the rebirth of brewpubs, establishments that brewed small amounts of beer on the premises. Sisson's, an establishment next to the city's Cross Street Market, became Maryland's first modern-era brewpub.

In his early days at the Cross Street restaurant, Sisson started off making ales, which took less time to produce, about two weeks rather than the six weeks needed to make lager. Sisson's Stockade—an ale with a gorgeous amber color and distinct yet balanced flavors—quickly appealed to beer drinkers who wanted more in their brew than the light, carbonated lagers being shipped into Baltimore from breweries in Milwaukee and St. Louis.

The brewpub filled up with customers eager to taste the variety of beer styles, from Stockade amber ale to the darker, sweeter Edgar Allan Porter. The operation soon developed into a center of beer-tasting research, where connoisseurs sniffed, sipped and enjoyed seasonal offerings such as Oktoberfest. The old European practice of brewing special beers at different seasons of the year began to take hold in Baltimore in the early 1990s, and Sisson was among the first to try it. The practice of brewing seasonal beers is now widespread among American craft brewers, such as Samuel Adams in Boston, which turns out beers for Oktoberfest and Christmas, as well as special brews for spring and summer. Like the characters in *Alice's Adventures in Wonderland* who celebrate "very merry unbirthdays," there seems to be a beer brewed for every turn of a calendar page.

Sisson's early brewing efforts did not always go smoothly. When he bollixed a batch of Raspberry Wheat beer by using the wrong yeast, he wanted to toss the beer out. But, as Sisson told a *City Paper* reporter in 2011, his dad talked him into serving it, and the bar patrons ended up guzzling it. "That was a mistake we got away with," Sisson told the reporter.

Sisson's served as host to another phenomenon, new in the '90s but common now: beer dinners. The tavern brought in chef Bill Aydlett, improved the bar's kitchen and, taking a page from wine dinners, had the restaurant chef match the courses of a meal with different styles of beer.

One occurred on a cool spring night in the mid-1990s. Six Baltimore-area brewers brought their beers to a dinner at Sisson's. As courses of the meal were served, various beers were poured. A series of brewers stood up and told the assembled diners interesting facts about their brews. As plates of oysters, clams and mussels poached in cream sauce circled the table, Mark Tewey—the youthful, lean, red-haired proprietor of Brimstone Brewing—entertained the crowd by describing the brewing process used to make Stone Beer, which accompanied the seafood course.

Tewey explained how he heated diabase rocks to 1,200 degrees and then dropped the hot rocks into a kettle of unfermented beer. The hot rocks caramelized sugars in the beer, he said, and gave it a sweet finish. Tewey, who began brewing beer a few years earlier in an apartment near Baltimore's Loyola College, took his higher education and extracurricular hobby to Brewers Hill in east Baltimore. There, in a portion of the

A Satisfying History of Charm City Brewing

building that once served as the home of National Premium and National Bohemian beers, Tewey ran his small brewery until 1994, when Frederick Brewing Company in Frederick, Maryland, acquired Brimstone. After a series of owners the Frederick brewery was sold in May 2006 to Flying Dog Brewing Company, which operates it today. Brimstone is no longer made at the brewery. Tewey also inspired his college roommate Dave Benfield to brew beer, and Benfield went on to found DuClaw Brewing Company in Harford County.

Sisson's early brewing setup on Cross Street was small, squeezed for space and required much manual labor. It had an annual capacity of 950 barrels. A canoe paddle, sanitized, was use to stir the brew. At the end of a brewing cycle, spent grain was shoveled from the bottom of the brew kettle, loaded into plastic trash cans and lugged by hand through a narrow corridor out to the alley. There it was sometimes set upon by "the twins," two south Baltimore vagabounds who had a taste for all things alcoholic.

After five years or so of this kind of beer making, Sisson yearned for something bigger, and in 1995 he moved from running a brewpub to a full-scale brewery. The brewery, set up in an industrial park in Halethorpe, was a short ride down Hollins Ferry Road from a massive, but no longer productive, Carling brewery. He named his brewery Clipper City after the speedy sailing ships that were built in Baltimore in the 1800s.

It was a slow start, and for a time Sisson was only able to keep his head above water by contract brewing, producing beer for other breweries. "At one point, 75 percent of the beer going out the door was other peoples' beer," Sisson told the *City Paper*. But he hung on and changed marketing tactics. In 2010, he rebranded his beers as Heavy Seas and divided them into three tiers, or fleets. The Clipper City Fleet has easy-drinking beers—Golden and Pale Ales, Marzen and Classic Lager—with low alcohol. The Pyrate Fleet is composed of more robust beers—Loose Cannon and Uber Pils—with higher alcohol. And its Mutiny Fleet—special issues, barley wines and imperial brews—are seasonal beers that come in twenty-two-ounce bottles and pack immense flavors.

The new strategy, combined with Sisson's persistent presence in the community—he leads weekend brewery tours, presides over beer dinners and serves as cohost of *Cellar Notes*, a weekly review of wines and beers on the local National Public Radio station—has yielded success. The brewery added a ten-thousand-square-foot addition to accommodate more brewing vessels and has an annual capacity of forty-five thousand barrels. It produces some twenty-one styles of ales and lagers, which are distributed in more than eighteen states. Its beers have won numerous medals at beer competitions, including five straight medals at the Great American Beer Festival in Denver, for its Marzen.

Just as Sisson followed in his father's footsteps when he took over the family pub in the 1980s, so has Patrick Dahlgren, Sisson's stepson. In early 2012, Dahlgren opened a two-hundred-seat beer-themed restaurant, the Heavy Seas Ale House, near the intersection of Bank Street and Central Avenue.

The new alehouse sits across the street from the old Canal Street Malt House. Built in 1866 on the road that was once called Canal Street but is now known as Central Avenue, the malt house, owned by Solomon Straus, was one of seven such facilities in the 1880s that provided malt to the city's many beer makers. Now, 156 years later, the old neighborhood got a new but historically correct resident, an alehouse where a young proprietor serves the beers made by his stepfather.

BALTIMORE BREWING COMPANY

Theo DeGroen attended that beer dinner at Sisson's in the mid-1990s. DeGroen, a dark-haired Dutchman, came to Baltimore from Holland, where his relatives brewed national favorite Grolsch beer. Arriving in December 1989, DeGroen set up his Baltimore Brewing Company brewery and restaurant at Albemarle and Lombard Streets, near the Flag House, where Mary Pickersgill stitched her place in history.

This was the second brewery in the city by that name. The original Baltimore Brewing Company in the 2200 block of West Pratt Street was run by Jacob Seeger, a brewer so well regarded that when he died in 1883, his funeral was attended by the reigning brewers of the day: Thomas Beck, J.H. von der Horst, John F. Wiessner Sr., George Bauernschmidt, Thomas M. Dukehart, Edward W. Stiefel, George Brehm and Henry Eigenbrot.

Seeger, like many of the early Baltimore brewers at his funeral, hailed from Germany. In the years preceding World War I, Baltimore was a very German community, a town bursting with Teutonic songfests and beer gardens. Some of that old-world flavor returned during the 1990s, when DeGroen opened the Baltimore Brewing Company.

Shortly after the gleaming copper kettles were installed in 1989, DeGroen began brewing lagers. His Marzen, Pils, Weizen and Doppelbock drew beer aficionados not just from the Baltimore area but from distant parts of Pennsylvania and northern Virginia as well.

A Satisfying History of Charm City Brewing

Using the refrigerated climes of a former food warehouse located next door, DeGroen turned out fresh, unfiltered brews. Later, some of these beers would be filtered and bottled, but many customers preferred to get their brews straight from the taps, having a mug or two at the bar and then filling up a growler with fresh beer to take home.

During the Friday happy hours in the 1990s, it was common to see a customer bid farewell to his colleagues and then depart carrying two, three or sometimes four growlers filled to the brim with Baltimore Brewing Company beer.

The brewery's handsome copper tanks served as a backdrop to a long bar. The bar looked out at the beer hall, filled with picnic tables and wooden stools. It was loud, it was crowded and it was fun. The kitchen served German-style fare, but the main attraction was the beer.

A Mug Club of some two hundred members regularly gathered at the brewery. Each member had a personal, numbered, one-liter glass stein that was stored when not in use on racks on the wall. Not only did these steins hold beer and carry status, but they also served as mailboxes. When members of the Mug Club wanted to communicate with one another, to invite folks to a party or to deliver tickets to an Orioles or Ravens game, they simply had the bartender drop the missives in the appropriate mug resting on the racks. Mug mail was a part of the Baltimore Brewing Company lifestyle.

The camaraderie led to field trips. In 1996, bartender Brad Plymale organized a trip to Victory Brewing Company in Downington, Pennsylvania, where Bill Covaleski and Ron Barchet, brewers who had once worked at the Baltimore Brewing Company, had set up operations. On a cold, dark February Monday, a rented bus, filled up with Baltimore Brewing Company regulars and with DeGroen himself, rolled out of Baltimore and headed north. After spending the day touring and sampling the fare at Victory, the Baltimore crew piled into the bus and returned home, en route sipping a few brews and watching the movie *Dr. Strangelove* on the bus's video system.

The brewery grew during the 1990s. In 1997, it was brewing six thousand barrels per year and aiming for fourteen thousand. But the Baltimore operation started to slip when DeGroen and his family moved to Germany, where he ran the Parkbaru Brewery in Rhineland-Pfalz and began splitting his attention between the Baltimore and German facilities. In February 2005, after fifteen years of brewing German-style beers that made men weep with joy, that helped transform scholarly librarians into high-fiving football fans and that encouraged city building inspectors to rub shoulders with professors, doctors and museum docents, the Baltimore Brewing Company stopped brewing. In making the announcement, DeGroen said that the only beer remaining was what was already kegged. Members of the Mug Club took it upon themselves to drain the last kegs. In remarks to a *Baltimore Sun* writer, they also reflected on the appeal of their doomed beer hall.

"The Baltimore Brewing Company and the Mug Club is a classic 'third place'—neither home nor work—where a true cross of section of Baltimore could socialize while enjoying great beer," said Brad Humphreys, who, along with his wife, Jane, were Mug Club members for twelve years before joining the faculty of the University of Illinois at Urbana–Champaign.

"Where else in town," Humphreys continued, "could you find a UMBC faculty member, a lifelong west side resident who works at the printing company and a pony-tailed biker from Arbutus debating anything from the U.S. Constitution to Mahler's symphonies?"

After Baltimore Brewing Company closed, some of its beers were bottled, for a time, by Fordham Brewing Company in Dover Delaware. The buildings on Albemarle and the adjacent Brewer's Park, site of some of the city's first breweries, were sold in 2007 to a Marriott hotel operation that erected the Fairfield Inn & Suites on the site.

Members of the Mug Club have an annual gathering at the Blue Hill Tavern in east Baltimore and try to satisfy their yearning for Baltimore Brewing Company's long-gone pils by sipping Victory Prima Pils, a beer, they report, is a close relative to the once fabled Baltimore pilsner.

Along with Sisson's, Baltimore Brewing Company helped revive the pre-prohibition practice of selling draught beer in growlers. These vessels—glassy variants on old metal buckets once used to carry beer—gave customers a way to tote draft beer home in something smaller than a barrel. Customers shelled out twelve dollars for the growler labeled with the brewery's name. Then they paid another seven dollars or so to have it filled up with the equivalent of almost a six-pack of beer. Once again, the sight of beer lovers toting large vessels of draft beer could be seen on the streets of Baltimore. The scene harkened back to the 1920s and '30s, when Baltimoreans got their beer in a bucket drawn from the tap at the corner tavern.

OLIVER BREWERIES AND THE PRATT STREET ALEHOUSE

As growler owners quickly learned, once their vessel was empty, it could be refilled with beer from another brewpub. Bill Oliver, then the proprietor of Oliver Breweries, a tidy operation set in middle of the Wharf Rat restaurant

A Satisfying History of Charm City Brewing

on Pratt Street, began getting occasional requests to fill up a Sisson's or Baltimore Brewing Company growler with one of the Oliver beers.

Baltimore is a marriage of the old and the new, and few brewing facilities have captured this union better than the Pratt Street Ale House. Sitting at 206 West Pratt Street, a few blocks north of the city's baseball and football stadiums and across the street from the Baltimore Convention Center, it is the city's oldest continually operating brewpub.

Its iron-front buildings erected in 1888 have turn-of-the-century touches, graceful old windows and tin ceilings, yet the establishment is festooned with twenty-five high-definition televisions, flashing the latest happenings in the modern world into the nineteenth-century setting.

The beers, English-style ales, emerge from a seven-barrel system tucked in the center of the alehouse. The brewing equipment, designed by Peter Austin, was imported from the United Kingdom and installed in 1993 by Oliver, the former proprietor, who grew up drinking the homemade beer made by his father, Harry, in their home in St. Catherine's, Ontario, and, as a result, developed a fondness for handcrafted ales. Oliver and his wife, Carole, sold the business to Donald Kelly and Justin Dvorkin in fall of 2008. The Oliver family shifted their focus to their Fells Point tavern, also known as the Wharf Rat.

In 2009, the new owners of the Pratt Street location spruced up the place but kept the establishment's emphasis on handcrafted ales and, more importantly, retained the services of Stephen Jones as brewmaster. A native of England, Jones has a deft touch with ales. A graduate of the University of Warwick, Coventry, United Kingdom, with a bachelor of science degree in biochemistry, Jones also has a diploma in brewing from the Institute of Brewing and Distilling, London. He brewed for the Firkin Brewery in Coventry and Loughborough in the United Kingdom for six years before joining Oliver Breweries in December 1999.

Some of the ales are cask-conditioned, a process that allows the unfiltered, unpasteurized brews to mature naturally, allowing live yeasts to produce mild, natural carbonation, giving the beers distinctive flavors. Moreover, several are hand-pumped, extracted from casks with a beer engine that uses a manual labor, not a modern gassy propellant, to deliver the beer to the tap. Some of its signature beers, such as its Extra Special Bitter, are served warm, or at least warmer than the usual chilled American beer. The warmer temperatures are said to bring out the flavors of the beer. Purists, such as the members of the Campaign for Real Ale, regard these techniques, with their roots in England, as superior. The local chapter of the Society for

Preservation of Beers from the Wood holds its annual October gathering at the Pratt Street Ale House.

When Oliver ran the establishment, he was especially pleased when a customer asked for one of the ales he serves at room temperature. Oliver liked to serve ale at fifty-four degrees and without artificial carbonation, as ale is sometimes served in England. Serving beer at this temperature, which is some fourteen degrees warmer than the forty-degree temperature of most American beers, heightens the beer's flavors, Oliver believes. Not everyone agreed with him—even members of the Oliver family who contributed to the brewing process preferred their ales cold and carbonated. So, the establishment adopted the "big tent" approach to beer making whereby all ale drinkers are welcome. Some of the ales are cold and carbonated; others are warm and cask-conditioned.

The alehouse sits in one of the oldest sections of Baltimore, and its various tenants over the years have reflected the changing makeup of the city's downtown. Initially, the structures at 202, 204 and 206 West Pratt Street served as homes for merchants who wanted to live near the city waterfront. As the city grew, the neighborhood became commercial, and the buildings were transformed to serve the Pratt Street Furniture Company. In 1980, as downtown Baltimore experienced a renaissance, the site became a restaurant, PJ Cricketts. It and its 1990s successor, the Wharf Rat, attracted tourists, convention goers and fans on their way to an Oriole or Ravens game.

Nowadays, the Pratt Street Ale House still draws the convention goers and sporting crowds, but it also attracts thirsty workers from the nearby University of Maryland hospital complex. There is also a new ale-drinking cohort, an increasing number of young professionals who reside in nearby lofts and condominiums. These new residents, like the nineteenth-century merchants, appreciate the downtown location and have a taste for tradition.

The Brewer's Art: Belgian Beers Even in a Can

It was quite a scene on the 1100 block of North Charles Street the day in 1996 when the massive front windows came off the gorgeous nineteenth-century mansion and brew kettles were squeezed in. That is how the Brewer's Art, a brewpub in Baltimore's Mount Vernon neighborhood specializing in hand-crafted Belgian-style beers, came to life.

A Satisfying History of Charm City Brewing

These feats of engineering—getting all the brewing equipment in also required removing a wall at the bottom of an elevator shaft—would, along with a quirk of nature, eventually produce what is arguably Baltimore's most popular craft beer, Resurrection Ale.

Belgian beers generally rely heavily on the yeast in the recipe, not just the malt or hops, to produce their distinctive and often adventurous flavors. This Belgian beer, Resurrection, gets its name from the fact that its yeast was born again. In 1997, Chris Cashell, then the brewer, was making a malty Belgian ale when it appeared that the yeast had died. Yeast converts sugar into alcohol, and when that process stops before the appointed time, brewers start worrying. Rather than tossing the batch out, Cashell recirculated the yeast, and miracle of miracles, the brew not only revived, but it also transformed into an amazingly smooth and malty brew.

Aptly named Resurrection, the ale, at 7 percent alcohol by volume, soon became a favorite of customers who frequented the North Charles Street location. Resurrection flowed freely both in the rathskeller, the dark basement bar popular with many students from the nearby University of Baltimore, and in the sunny, marble-endowed upstairs bar, filled with thirsty lawyers, writers and former squash stars. The upstairs bar leads into a stately turn-of-the-century dining room, and local critics have rated its work as one of the city's top dining venues. Yet beer was primarily responsible for the Brewer's Art reputation. Locally, it has became regarded as one of the area's best brewpubs, and Resurrection is a top-selling beer at Max's Taphouse, Pratt Street Ale House and other craft beer–oriented bars around town, including a string of taverns and restaurants in Lauraville. This neighborhood in northeast Baltimore is filled with establishments, such as the Hamilton Tavern, Chameleon Café and Clementine, run by Brewer's Art alumni, men and women who once worked at the brewpub and still like the beer.

Over the last fifteen years, Brewer's Art has built a national reputation as well. It has twice been named one of the best bars in America by *Esquire* magazine, and *Imbibe* magazine has named it one of the best one hundred places in America to drink beer.

Even though it is now popular, Resurrection was, at its inception, a beer running against a trend. It had a strong malty profile—five different malts go into the recipe—and while it had hops, it avoided the widespread practice of pouring in excessive amounts of hops.

"For years, the idea among some craft brewers was that hops were the source of all flavor, so people would hop the daylights out of beer," Volker

Stewart, co-owner of the Brewer's Art told *Baltimore Magazine* in October 2010. "I think by eliminating that as the driving force in your beer, you can really open your market up."

Demand for Resurrection and other Brewer's Art beer is so strong that the eight-and-a-half-barrel brewery runs at capacity. Stewart regularly gets telephone calls and text messages from tavern owners asking for kegs of Resurrection. He puts them on a waiting list.

To widen their market, Stewart and co-owner Tom Creegan, took the leap in 2008 of putting some of their beers—Green Peppercorn Tripel, Le Canard, Resurrection, Ozzy and La Petroleuse—in 750ml bottles for sale in area liquor stores. The bottling was done in an arrangement with Sly Fox Brewery in Royersford, Pennsylvania, which brews and packages the beers.

Then, in 2010, the Brewer's Art owners took another leap, packaging Resurrection in six-packs of twelve-ounce cans. This, too, was done with Sly Fox. The practice of putting craft beer in cans had been pioneered by Oskar Blues, a Colorado brewer, yet it was a gamble.

"We weren't sure it would work," Stewart said. "The perception of canned beer as cheap beer was out there, but over time it has faded. If we had tried canning Resurrection five years earlier, it might not have succeeded." Now, he said, the demand for canned beer is constantly growing. Since cans are recycled, canned beer, he said, is viewed as ecologically sound and "very green."

A college graduate with degrees in history and library science, Stewart contends that much of the popularity of craft beers stems from demographics. He noted that his generation—the beer-loving age group from thirty to forty-nine—was the first to have grown up in America with craft beer. Stewart came to Baltimore from Seattle in 1991. "Ever since I got out of college, the number of craft breweries has increased," he said. Consequently, his generation is comfortable with having a wide variety of craft beers to choose from, even if some of these elixirs come in cans, vessels once thought of as the carriers of only inexpensive, blue-collar brews.

Flying Dog Arrives from Colorado

Flying Dog Brewery, like many residents of Maryland, hails from another state, moving to Frederick, Maryland, in stages, starting in 2006 and completing the transition in 2008. It has been a welcome addition.

A Satisfying History of Charm City Brewing

Flying Dog started as a brewpub in Aspen, Colorado, in 1990. In 1994, it began bottling at Broadway Brewing in Denver, Colorado, in what was once the Silver State Laundry building, an establishment that was the favored laundry of prostitutes who once serviced the area's silver miners, or so the story goes.

Broadway Brewing was a 50/50 joint venture between the Wynkoop Brewing Company and Flying Dog. In 1999, Broadway Brewing moved its operation to a larger facility about two blocks away, and shortly thereafter, Flying Dog bought out the Wynkoop interest in the brewery and renamed it the Flying Dog Brewery.

Even so, it could not keep with the demand for its beers, much of it coming from East Coast drinkers. So it made the jump to Maryland, acquiring a nine-year-old brewery in Frederick, a structure that originally was built for the Frederick Brewing Company, a brewery that had a sad fate.

The owners of Frederick Brewing Company ended up selling their brewery, the largest in the state of Maryland. In 1993, Frederick began brewing its Blue Ridge line of beers. In 1994, it expanded and soon absorbed Mark Tewey's Brimstone beers, as well as Wild Goose Brewery, the Cambridge, Maryland operation that since 1989 had brewed highly regarded ales.

The expanded Frederick brewery added a number of new beers to its line of products, including Hempen Ale, a brew made with hemp (a legal relative of marijuana). Frederick also considered bringing back an old Baltimore favorite—National Premium. At a May 1999 press conference presided over by former Maryland governor and Baltimore mayor William Donald Schaefer—who claimed that he didn't drink beer but did like to promote Maryland businesses—officials of the Frederick brewery passed out samples of the resurrected National Premium. They claimed that the resurrected brew would be on sale in the coming summer months. However, those plans went on hold as the struggling brewer saw its stock price fall to a fraction of its original value, and the company was acquired in late 1999 by C. David Snyder, a computer software businessman from Ohio. Eventually, Flying Dog got the brewery in bankruptcy court.

For a few years, Flying Dog was a bi-state operation, brewing in both Colorado and Maryland, but by January 2008, all beers were coming out of the Frederick plant. In addition to Flying Dog, the Frederick operation brewed beers for Wild Goose, Crooked River and Blue Ridge but eventually shed those obligations. In 2011, it produced about 90,000 barrels of beer, or about double the capacity of the brewery when Flying Dog took it over. Its total capacity is currently 115,000 barrels.

Now some thirty different bottled beers come out of Flying Dog, wrapped in more than one hundred different packages. A small canning line is slated to begin in 2012, putting the brewery's Snake Dog IPA and Under Dog, a new 4.7 percent ABV "Atlantic Lager," in cans. "We are a regional brewery," Jim Caruso, the brewery's chief executive officer, said, "an inch wide and a mile deep."

Bowing to demand, the brewery is offering an increasing number of tours of its Frederick plant. Caruso, the CEO, sometimes leads the tours. "I love showing people the brewery, explaining the brewery process and especially tasting beers with the tour groups," he said.

While the Flying Dog Brewery has roots in Colorado, its name comes from Pakistan. That is where George Stranahan—the brewery's founder (and who has a PhD in physics), founder of the Aspen Institute for Physics, professional photographer, writer and heir to the Champion Spark Plug fortune—spotted a painting in one of the rooms at Flashman's Hotel Rawalpindi in 1983.

Stranahan was parched after he and his group of thirteen "innocents" crossed the Braldu Gorge and Baltoro Glacier on a trek toward the summit of K2. After signing a document saying that he was a Christian and that his father was a Christian—Muslins in Pakistan were forbidden to drink alcohol, but Christians were cleared—Stranahan secured beer for the group.

A painting in one of the rooms captured his imagination. It was an oil painting of a dog that resembled a Brittany spaniel, coming off the ground in a twisted fashion with its front legs outstretched, its ears blown back and its back legs tucked up underneath it as if it were about to take off from the ground like Superman. As best they could figure, a local artist misunderstood the concept of an English bird dog and imagined that there were dogs in England that could fly.

Stranahan was fixated on the painting and eventually named it *Flying Dog*. Stranahan was so taken with image that once he returned home to Woody Creek, Colorado he began applying the "Flying Dog" appellation to his holdings, first renaming his ranch the Flying Dog Ranch (it had been called the Lower Collins Creek Coyote Preserve). When he started a brewpub in Aspen, Colorado, it had to be called the Flying Dog brewpub.

Stranahan was a friend of the writer Hunter S. Thompson and artist Ralph Steadman, who illustrated all of Hunter's works beginning in 1970. Steadman began doing original art for Flying Dog in 1997, and his artwork appears on the brewery's extremely colorful, if sometimes hard to read, Flying Dog labels.

A Satisfying History of Charm City Brewing

DuClaw Brewing Company, Harford County

When he was in college, Dave Benfield, founder of DuClaw Brewing Company, did not exactly major in beer, but he spent a lot of time thinking about it. He and his roommate, Mark Tewey, did brew beer in their Loyola College apartment. Tewey later opened Brimstone Brewing, a short-lived operation located on Brewers Hill and based on the premise that dropping hot rocks into beer made it taste better.

Benfield stayed interested in brewing, and in 1996, four years after he graduated from Loyola, he opened DuClaw as a brewery and restaurant in Bel Air. Benfield's first batch of beer was supposed to be a malty Marzen, but he was not familiar with the gas burner of the brew kettle, and it boiled over, so he had to add water, creating what he called a "Helles-style brew," a watery brew he admits he wouldn't sell today.

In the early days, Benfield brewed a blonde ale, a brown ale, a blackberry wheat beer and a porter. Now DuClaw has six to seven mainstays, adds one or two new beers per month and produces about twenty-two to twenty-four different beers a year.

An avid comic book collector, Benfield draws may of the names of his beers, such as Serum, from the comics. The racy name for one of his beers, Bare Ass Blonde, was the result, he said, of a dare. A friend of the family dared him to give the beer that moniker, and Benfield rose to the challenge, even though his mother did not approve.

Benfield is a fan of growlers. DuClaw has tried out several varieties of the containers. DuClaw also has a bottling line in its Abdington plant in Harford County. It has acquired a larger facility in Havre de Grace, and when it moves there, it can expand its capacity up to 125,000 barrels per year.

His beers, Benfield says, have "strong personalities" and usually high alcohol content. DuClaw's Devil's Milk is 11 percent alcohol by volume. The key to success when dealing with such big beers, Benfield says, is to maintain balance of flavors. He also is a proponent of beer education and entertainment. Each new beer that DuClaw releases is accompanied by notes on the brewery's website describing the brew, as well as by a video of having fun with the new arrival.

Whether it is propaganda or education, the approach seems to be working. DuClaw has four area restaurants—in Bel Air, Bowie, Arundel Mills and at the Baltimore Washington International Thurgood Marshall Airport—that serve its brews.

DuClaw, which began as a Harford County brewpub, now has an extensive bottling operation. *Courtesy DuClaw.*

When DuClaw opened back in the 1990s, the twentysomethings who frequented its restaurant drank mainly Coors Light. Lately, members of the same age group are not only sipping more complex brews, like the double India Pale Ale, they are also critiquing them, telling Benfield, the onetime college brewer, what he is doing right.

Brewer's Alley, Monocacy: A Brewery Bets Bigger

In 2012, six-packs of bottled beer from Monocacy Brewing Company in Frederick began arriving in Baltimore liquor stores. These beers were an outgrowth of Brewer's Alley, a restaurant and brewpub owned by Phil Bowers and operated in downtown Frederick.

For years, Tom Flores, the brewer at Brewer's Alley, had been content to make beers that slaked the thirst of customers who patronized the restaurant and brewpub. From the mid-1990s to 2010, Flores made several interesting beers, including a remarkably crisp Kolsch and an ale named 1634. It was made with molasses, malted wheat and caraway and used a recipe that,

A Satisfying History of Charm City Brewing

as best Flores could determine, was similar to the one Maryland's first colonizers enjoyed. These beers were sold on tap in kegs, and some were bottled by another brewer. But outside Frederick, Brewer's Alley beers were hard to find.

That changed in late 2011, when Bowers moved the bulk of the brewing operation to a former Ebert Ice Cream factory two miles north of downtown Frederick and inaugurated Monocacy Brewing Company, a twenty-five-barrel plant with its own bottling line. Bottles of its initial offering, a rye-based India Pale Ale from Monocacy, sold out in Baltimore shops.

Brewer Flores is quite familiar with the Baltimore brewing scene. After college at the University of California–Davis, Flores brewed for Clipper City Brewing Company in Baltimore County, Hugh Sisson's operation that now produces beers under the Heavy Seas label.

When Flores moved to Brewer's Alley in the mid-1990s, the craft beer scene in Frederick was pretty quiet. Over the years, interest grew, thanks in part to the presence of the Flying Barrel, a shop that encouraged and supplied home brewers. That shop relocated in 2012, moving into space in the new Monocacy brewery.

The arrival of the Flying Dog Brewery also spurred local curiosity about beer making. At the same time, Frederick's dining scene began heating up when the Voltaggio brothers, Bryan and Michael, natives of Frederick, won national attention for themselves and their hometown when they garnered honors competing on the television program *Iron Chef*. Volt, the James Beard Award–winning restaurant in downtown Frederick where Bryan Voltaggio is the executive chef, is so popular that would-be customers make reservations weeks in advance for an open table.

Local brewers have capitalized on the increased interest in fine food and drinking, organizing dinners that matched the work of the city's budding chefs with its brewers. Barley and Hops, another local brewpub, joined the ranks of Frederick brewers in 1999. Lately, brewery tours have become an attraction, a way to spend an afternoon in Frederick. "Once people are introduced to the world of craft beers," Flores said, "there is no turning back."

One reason that craft breweries are flourishing in Frederick is its strategic location. Sitting at the top of a triangle of interstate highways with Baltimore and Washington at its base, Frederick is a short distance from both major markets. While the connecting highways can get clogged, the location is nonetheless prime. When Flores needs a batch of yeast to start a brew, he can order it from distant vendors and know that thanks to the nearby airports in Baltimore and Washington, it will arrive overnight. Another factor for

Flores is the good local water supply. Water pulled from Lake Linganore, the Monocacy River and the reservoir west of Frederick is plentiful and dependable—vital to brewing.

While the local climate is not ideal for producing hops, barley does grow in western Maryland, and Flores has had some success using malt made from the local crop. As Monocacy grows, Flores plans to expand the use of locally grown ingredients in his beers.

Monocacy makes six beers year round and adds another five seasonal offerings. Ever the experimenter, Flores made a beer for the brewery's tenth anniversary that drew components from the fifty beers he brewed in the operation's first decade. "It was a super complex beer fermented as an ale," he said. "I was worried that with all those flavors it could be muddy, but it worked out well."

Rams Head and Fordham Mix Beer and Music

In the early 1990s, a brewpub in Annapolis began mixing Maryland tradition with live music. The result was the Rams Head Fordham Brewing Company enterprise. In Baltimore's Inner Harbor, there are two spots, Rams Head Live in the Power Plant building and the Pier 6 outdoor pavilion, where the happy confluence of bands and brews meet.

As the music plays, beers from Fordham's brewery in Dover, Delaware, are served on tap. In addition to these two Baltimore concert sites, Fordham brews are also poured at a Rams Head concert spot in Annapolis. The concert sites vary in size: Annapolis can handle a crowd of a little over three hundred, while Pier 6 can accommodate four thousand. Rams Head also operates four restaurants in Savage, Crownsville, Stevenson and Rehoboth, Delaware. At the restaurants, however, the musical performances are more casual, with no tickets needed.

The lineage of this brewing operation goes back to 1703, when Benjamin Fordham established a commercial brewery, the first in colonial Maryland, in Annapolis. Fast forward to 1988, when William Muehlhauser bought the Rams Head Tavern in Annapolis. In 1995, Muehlhauser and his son, Kyle, began brewing beer there, naming their operation Fordham in honor of the colonial brewer.

Fordham made ales and lagers, and demand for them was strong. In 2003, the brewing activity moved to a larger site, a twenty-two-thousand-barrels-per-year facility in Dover, Delaware. Here the four main line

A Satisfying History of Charm City Brewing

Fordham beers—Copperhead Ale, Tavern Ale, Helles and Light Lager—are produced year round. Four seasonal brews—Wisteria Wheat, Scotch Ale, Spcied Harvest Ale and Doppelbock—are each produced for a few months of the year. All of the beers are put in kegs. The seasonal beers and three mainstays—Tavern Ale, Helles and Copperhead Ale, which in 2009 was named by Yahoo.com as one of the top ten American pale ales—are bottled.

Fordham formed a joint venture with Anheuser-Busch called Coastal Brewing Company and, in March 2007, bought Old Dominion Brewing Company of Ashburn, Virginia. The Old Dominion beers are brewed and bottled at Fordham's Delaware brewery.

WHITE MARSH BREWING COMPANY: CRAFT BEER IN THE SUBURBS

On Tuesdays in White Marsh, beer drinkers looking for bargains are likely to gather at the Red Brick Station restaurant, home of the White Marsh Brewing Company in the Baltimore County suburbs northeast of Baltimore.

Tuesdays are sale days, for most of the ales made at this brewpub. They go for one dollar a glass. There are exceptions. Seasonal brews, for example, go for two dollars. But the main line brews of this operation, the Avenue Ale, Honeygo Lite, Daily Crisis IPA, Something Red and Spooner's Stout, are served up for a buck.

On Tuesday evenings, a crowd rings the bar of the Red Brick Station. The restaurant, built to resemble a firehouse, sits on the Avenue, a collection of stores that resemble a Main Street in small-town America. The dollar beer night has been a tradition at Red Brick Station since the late 1990s, almost as long as Mike McDonald, the brewmaster of White Marsh Brewing Company, has been making beers on the premises.

McDonald came to White Marsh in 1997 from Derry, New Hampshire, where he had worked at the Old Nutfield Brewery. McDonald has a taste for English ales, beers of relatively mild alcohol—most 3 to 4 percent by volume—and smooth, melded flavors.

McDonald was hired by owners Bill Blocher and Tony Meoli, two local businessmen who believed that the fast-growing suburbs were ready for a brewpub. Figuring that the patrons would be drawn to more nuanced beers rather than extreme brews, McDonald aimed at creating a line of "session" beers, ones that in the English tradition could be enjoyed without being overwhelmed by alcohol.

Mike McDonald, brewmaster at White Marsh Brewing Company in the Red Brick Station Restaurant. *Courtesy White Marsh.*

He figured right. His 14-barrel operation, set up just inside the entrance of the restaurant yields an annual output of almost 1,600 barrels. The most popular beer is the Daily Crisis India Pale Ale, a brew he named after a dairy farm, Daily Crisis, in nearby White Hall, Maryland. Dairy cows, like brewers, treasure consistency and get upset when the routine is broken, McDonald explained. In addition, the cows at this farm dine on the spent grain from the brewery.

McDonald has been known to brew on the wild side. Each spring since 1998, he has mixed wild blueberries with an ale to create a special seasonal brew. McDonald claims not to be a fan of fruit-flavored beers, and when it first appeared, McDonald feigned reluctance and dubbed the brew the They-Made-Me-Do-It Blueberry Ale. But it sells well, and like the dollar beers on Tuesday, it has become a tradition. Moreover, in an unguarded moment, McDonald will admit that he actually likes it.

A Satisfying History of Charm City Brewing

DOG Brewing Company, Westminister

There was a time in George Humbert's life when he lived in Bethesda yet traveled forty miles to Baltimore to drink beer.

His destination in those days of the early 1990s was Sisson's in Baltimore's Federal Hill neighborhood, the state's first brewpub. There he downed glasses of Marble Golden Ale and was taken with its subtle flavors. That ale started Humbert, now the proprietor of DOG Brewing Company in Westminster, on the road to craft brewing. Or, as he put it, "I was hooked." When more craft brewers, such as the Wharf Rat and Baltimore Brewing Company, opened their taps in Baltimore, Humbert was there as well, sampling the goods.

About the same time, he discovered home brewing. "I called a buddy of mine and asked what he was doing, and he said, 'Brewing a batch of beer,'" Humbert recalled. "I said, 'I'll be right over!' I watched him brew, and then we drank it several weeks later. It was one of those 'Eureka' moments."

After college (he graduated from Boston University in 1993), Humbert put in a four-year stint at the Olde Towne Tavern and Brewery in Gaithersburg, learning the brewing craft and brewpub business and meeting his business partner Steve Osmond. They eventually bought a shuttered bar on Cross Street in Baltimore, renovated the building and opened Thirsty Dog Pub a few doors down from the old Sisson's brewpub, which had since changed hands and stopped brewing. At the Thirsty Dog, Humbert sold craft beers, sourced from local Old Dominion Brewing Company in Ashburn, Virginia.

Then, in 2006, thanks to a combination of love, marriage and luck, Humbert founded DOG Brewing Company and started brewing again fulltime. He and his wife were about to be blessed with twin girls, Kristin and Grace, and his wife did not want him spending his nights in the pub, Humbert said, explaining the love and marriage components. Luck figured into the equation when Gregg Norris wanted to sell the Clay Pipe Brewery that Norris had built in Westminster in 2001.

Humbert took over the brewery, christened it DOG in honor of his Federal Hill pub and began making a line of American ales. He likes to keep his beers simple. "I am a big fan of old-school American taverns like McSorley's (Old Ale House) in New York, and I want to make beers both balanced and sessionable that would fit in there," he said.

The brewery yields thirty-barrel batches. He brews about five thousand barrels per year, turning out eleven different types of ale. Much of the beer is kegged and goes to two Pub Dog Pizza & Drafthouses, one on Cross Street, formally known as the Thirsty Dog, and the other in Columbia, Maryland.

In 2009, Humbert, using a manual bottle filler, began putting his DOG ales in 750mL bottles, which are sold in area liquor stores. In 2011, he bought a used automated bottling line from a German brewer to keep up with demand.

Bottling is often a headache for brewers, and Humbert likened his vintage bottling equipment to a German car. "It is like an old diesel Mercedes," he said. "It can be a little cranky in the morning, but if you take care of it, it will run forever."

JOHANSSON'S WESTMINSTER, MARYLAND

At Johansson's Dining House and brewpub in Westminster, freight trains play a role in making the beer.

The scenic restaurant holding a seven-barrel brewery sits right next to railroad tracks. When Maryland Midland Railway freight trains come rolling through town, the entire brewery vibrates. Brewer Jay Lampart speculates that the shaking stimulates the yeast in the brew, giving what he calls a "personal taste to the beer."

Not surprisingly, one of the beers brewed at this quaint Carroll County spot is called Whistle Stop Amber. As is true with the many mysteries of beer making, the exact effect that the freight train rumble has on the brew is matter of some discussion. Some days, three trains roll past the brewpub, and other days there are none. Yet the Whistle Stop Amber regularly emerges from the tanks as a ruby-red ale with cascade hops and malty sweetness.

Since its inception in 1998, this brewing operation has had a strong, local, almost neighborly feel to it. Take, for instance, the name of its most popular beer, Hoodle Head India Pale Ale. The name, as proprietor Dave Johansson explained to a *Baltimore Sun* reporter in 2000, goes back to the days when Johansson was a student at Hereford High School in Baltimore County. When someone misbehaved, he was called a "hoodle head," Johansson said.

Johansson liked the term so much that when he married and had children, he and his wife sometimes called their offspring "hoodle heads." Then, when Johansson opened the brewing operation and got a chance to name a beer hoodle head, he couldn't pass it up.

Lampart, who took over brewing operations in 2005, also has a penchant for personalizing the names of his beers. He has named two of seasonal beers after his two young daughters, Olivia and Katelyn. A native of New York City whose grandfather once worked on the bottling line at the F. and

A Satisfying History of Charm City Brewing

M. Schaefer plant there, Lampart came to Baltimore to study the hospitality industry at the Baltimore International College. He got a job as a line cook at Caves Valley Golf Club and later was promoted to pastry chef. In addition to his cooking duties, Lampart began working as assistant brewer at Johannson's. When in 2005 the operation's first brewer, Joe McGonagle, moved on, Lampart took over.

His main line of beers, the Hoodle Head IPA, the Whistle Stop and a golden ale called Honest Ale, are English-style brews. "I like to make session beers, beers with 5 to 6 alcohol by volume, beers I like to drink," he said. The beers are served on tap and sold in growlers.

He branches out when making seasonal or one-of-a-kind beers. In 2012, he made a Belgian-style brew, a bigger beer, 8.4 percent alcohol by volume. The beer, named Reason Saison, was a tribute to Ron Smith, the host of a daily talk show on WBAL radio who died in late 2011.

On tap are Lampart's plans to brew an ale for the Caves Valley Club, where he still works as pastry chef. The beer will be served on tap both in the club dining room and on the golf course, at an oasis between the ninth and tenth holes.

Ellicott Mills:
A Taste of Germany in Howard County

Tucked in a stone building in downtown Ellicott City just west of Baltimore, the Ellicott Mills Brewing Company, a brewpub and restaurant, has been making German-style brews since 1997.

It hasn't always been easy. Tim Kendzierski and the other owners have battled the elements. A burst water main delayed Ellicott Mills opening in 1997, and heavy rains in 2011 filled the basement with several feet of water. But weather and roiling waters could not keep the brewer from making his appointed beers, and with a German-style determination, Ellicott Mills has continued to produce brews.

Its lagers and ales have won medals in local beer competitions, and brewer Ray Andreassen is especially proud of the brewery's line of bock beers. Bock beer is a rich, malty lager low in hops. Because it has higher nutritional content than other beers, bock was once used by German monks during their Lenten fast as a liquid substitute for food. "Bock was fortifying," Andreassen said.

In Baltimore in 1950s and '60s, bock beers made by National, Gunther and American breweries traditionally appeared in the spring, often

The rollout of bock beer, a strong lager (curiously associated with goats), was a popular springtime ritual in post–World War II Baltimore and remains strong today in Ellicott City. *Photo by Jim Burger.*

advertised with posters that showed a dancing goat. The word *bock* means goat in German. But according to Andreassen, the regional accent of some Bavarians also figured in linking bock with goats. The German town of Einbeck is believed to be where the beer originated. When the residents of this region of Bavaria pronounced the name of the town, they made it sound like *ein bock*, which means billy goat, hence the connection.

There is a more colorful, if historically questionable, story linking bock beer and goats. The story, founded on Cincinnati's Bockfest website, goes that long ago two bock-brewing German monks were having a beer-drinking contest in a tavern. Bock beers have a high alcohol content, usually 6 to 12 percent, but some can go as high as 43 percent. After downing several bock beers, the loser of the competition fell over. He blamed his downfall on an errant goat that had wandered into the tavern. The victor looked down at his prostrate drinking companion and told him that the only goat that had knocked him down was the beer.

There are several styles of bock at Ellicott Mills. Maibocks, or Helles, are paler than other bocks and are hoppy. Doppelbock is malty, dark and strong. Eisbock is a muscle beer and can have a strong alcohol taste.

Andreassen touted the bocks of Ellicott Mills Brewing Company in an appearance in *Brewed on the Bay*, the 2011 Maryland Public Television documentary written by Al Spoeler that profiled the state's craft beer industry. "We always have a bock on tap," he said. Ellicott Mills, he continued, "produces more types of bock beer than any American brewery." Accordingly, the stone brewery building in downtown Ellicott City is known by patrons as the "House of Bock."

EVOLUTION CRAFT BREWING COMPANY: FROM THE SHORE TO THE CITY

Evolution Craft Brewing, one of the state's newer breweries, is based on the Eastern Shore yet it has ample ties to and taps in Baltimore.

Tommy Knorr, the brewery's cofounder, went to McDonogh High School outside Baltimore, and his brother and business partner, John, is an executive with Phillips Seafood restaurants. When customers come to a Phillips restaurant in Baltimore, Washington or Ocean City craving seafood and beer, Evolution beers are there to greet them.

Founded in 2009 by the Knorr brothers, the brewery took over an old grocery store in Delmar, Delaware, just north of the Maryland line. They hired Geoff DeBisschop from John Harvard's Brewhouse in Cambridge, Massachusetts, as their brewmaster and started off making low-alcohol, food-friendly ales. "Rather than a hop monster, we want well-balanced beers that aren't going to bash you," Tommy Knorr told a *Sun* reporter in August 2009.

Their ales, especially the Exile ESB (Extra Special Bitter), soon found friends, and the small ten-barrel brewery and tasting room on Bi-Coastal Highway was humming and occasionally steaming as it turned out fresh beer. One summer night, some of their customers arrived at the brewery in cars and others wheeled in "cowboy Cadillacs" pickup trucks. They left with a growler or two of fresh beer.

In addition to selling beer in kegs, the brewery put in a bottling line, and six-packs of their main line beers have shown up in liquor stores throughout the state. Evo brews five main line beers—a pale ale, an extra special bitter, a porter, an IPA and a stout—year round in bottles and kegs. Four seasonal beers, one each in the fall, spring, winter and summer, join the main line beers in the market. Lately, barrel-aged brews—beers aged in wine, bourbon or rum barrels—have been added to the lineup.

Demand for Evo's beer has grown, and in 2012 it opened a new forty-barrel brewery and restaurant in Salisbury.

Brewers on the Move: Stillwater's Brian Strumke and the Raven's Stephen Demczuk

Some craft brewers who don't have their own brick-and-mortar operations lease space from existing breweries. Baltimore has two such brewers who have established good reputations for their beers.

Brian Strumke grew up in east Baltimore, in the shadow of the old National Brewing Company. Now in his thirties, he is a self-styled gypsy brewer, traveling the world to make his Belgian-style ales known as Stillwater Artisanal Ales. He brews some of his beers at DOG Brewery in Westminster, but he also leases space and time at breweries in Belgium and central Europe. In 2010, for instance, he made beer in seven breweries in three countries. He garnered national acclaim in 2011 when the website Rate Beer named him the second-best new brewer in the world. Top honors went to Hill Farmstead Brewery in Greensboro, Vermont.

Strumke was drawn to beer making when his work as a producer and disc jockey of techno music events in Europe began to slow down. "I started getting really bored," he told the *Sun* in 2010. "I was used to traveling in Europe and playing music. I needed a creative outlet."

A native of east Baltimore, he graduated from Archbishop Curley High School, and over the years he took classes at Dundalk and Essex Community Colleges and at Johns Hopkins University, where for a time he worked as an information technology staffer. But college, he said, did not suit him, and when his music career slacked off, he "took stock of my life…looking for something I could put my energy in."

He borrowed a home-brewing kit from his friend, Graham Bouton. He got help from local home-brewing groups such as the Chesapeake Real Ale Brewers Society and the Cross Street Irregulars. He entered a few of his home brews, a dark Belgian with molasses and ginger and a Cabernet Sauvignon lambic, in competitions sponsored by the American Homebrewers Association and the Samuel Adams brewery in Boston. He won ribbons and a free trip to the Great American Beer Festival in Denver.

One night in Baltimore, he persuaded Brian Ewing, founder of 12 Percent Imports, a Brooklyn, New York–based distributor, to taste his beers. Ewing liked what he tasted. Strumke worked a deal with DOG Brewing Company to give him some time in the brewery, and his commercial career began. Strumke blends unusual ingredients, like dandelion, lavender and chamomile, into Belgian-style beers. He sees his brewing "as much as an artistic endeavor as a business."

A Satisfying History of Charm City Brewing

In a 2010 review in the *Washington Post* of Strumke's beers, Greg Kitsock observed that "most Beer 101 books peg saison as a specific beer style, but Strumke sees it as more of a concept."

"Almost every farmhouse in Belgium had a brewery attached to it," Strumke told the *Post*. "When they weren't farming, they were brewing. And every farm had a different style. They used whatever ingredients they had. If they had a lot of wheat or spelt or oats, they used that. If they had no hops, they used spices."

Strumke's credo is that brewing "is a mixture of chemistry and art" and that "a brewer does not always have to play by the rules."

In 2012, Strumke made a move toward setting up a brick-and-mortar headquarters, opening a pub, Of Love & Regret, on Conkling Street in Brewers Hill. The pub, a partnership with restaurateur Ted Stelzenmuller, will serve Strumke's ales on draft.

THE RAVEN SPECIAL LAGER

In 1996, a National Football League team came to Baltimore from Cleveland, and in Europe, Baltimore native Stephen Demczuk struck a deal with a German brewer to produce new beer. Both the football barons and the beer broker turned to the work of Baltimore's famous poet, Edgar Allan Poe, for inspiration. Both ended up naming their enterprises after Poe's 1845 poem, "The Raven."

Since then, the Baltimore Ravens football team has enjoyed great success, winning the Super Bowl in 2000 and making repeated appearances in the postseason playoffs. The Raven beer, a lager, has become a local favorite, especially during football season, even though there is no commercial connection between the beer and the team. Raven beer was sold for two years, 1998 and 1999, in M&T Bank Stadium, where the team plays, but when the stadium changed caterers, it was dropped.

In the mid-1990s, Demczuk was living in Luxembourg when the beer was born. He was part of a company called Beer Around the World, which shipped beers to connoisseurs in fifteen countries. In 1996, he and a partner, Wolfgang Stark, struck a deal with a brewery in Nagold, Germany, to make a beer that would be sold both in Europe and in the Baltimore metropolitan area. They called their beer the Raven because, Demczuk said, research showed that in the minds of European beer drinkers, "Baltimore was famous for two things, Edgar Allan Poe and 'The Star-Spangled Banner.'" Given those two options, Demczuk went with the poet.

European beer drinkers also didn't know much about American geography. They weren't sure where Baltimore was, so Demczuk tossed a "Washington" into the title of his company that went on the beer label, calling it the Baltimore-Washington Beer Works. In 1998, after Demczuk and his family moved back to the Baltimore area, he brewed the Raven at the Baltimore County brewery Clipper City Brewing Company.

Demczuk grew up in Dundalk, graduated from Patapsco High School and the University of Maryland and achieved a doctorate in biochemistry and molecular biology from the University of Oklahoma. For years he drank mainstream American beer. His conversion to craft beer occurred in 1983 when he was in a pub in Mainz, Germany. At a colleague's suggestion, he ordered a glass of Pilsner Urquell, a Czech lager. When the beer arrived in a regal, pilsener-style glass, with its creamy head, aroma and complex flavor, it bowled him over. "It was a near-religious experience," Demczuk told a reporter for the *Baltimore Sun* in a 2002 interview. Demczuk's interest in beer blossomed. While continuing to work in molecular biology, he sipped European brews, became a correspondent for *American Brewer* magazine and later got into the beer distribution business.

In 2010, the Raven finished in the finals of a beer madness competition run by the *Washington Post*, modeled after college basketball's March Madness tournament and described as a quest to find Everyman's favorite brew. The Raven Special Lager finished in the top four beers, winnowed from a field of thirty-two beers, but was bested in the semifinals by Samuel Smith Oatmeal Stout, the eventual champion.

Demczuk has always been proud of his beer. During a lunch in a downtown Baltimore hotel in 2002, Demczuk held up a glass of Raven beer and beamed like an exultant father. "The Munich malt gives it that sweetness," he said. Four hops, including a full-flower Saaz hop, are used in the beer, he said, along with German yeast. The lager is 5.5 percent alcohol by volume. "I wanted a rich amber color, not black, with a nice aroma, something like Samuel Adams but with a taste and body that makes it very drinkable."

In 2012, Demczuk began exploring the possibility of a cooperative venture with two other brewers. The coop, known as Charm City Brewing Company, would brew and bottle in a building on the 400 block of East Thirtieth Street in Waverly.

A Satisfying History of Charm City Brewing

The Future of Suds City

In some ways, Baltimore's beer-making business has come full circle. Back when Baltimore was little more than a series of brick buildings near the water, the beer business was a locally based enterprise. Over the years, it grew, with large breweries rising along Gay Street and on Brewers Hill in east Baltimore. For a time, National Brewing Company (the king of Brewers Hill) dominated the city and cultivated a national reputation as one of America's premium beers. Then, as interstate highways and television advertising transformed the beer business from a local to a national undertaking, larger out-of-state brewers swooped in and swallowed up local breweries, including the once regal National.

Eventually, the big national brewers, troubled by stagnant sales, closed up their major Baltimore breweries. But as tarnished brewing tanks were yanked out of old breweries, like Carling in Halethorpe, newer and smaller brewing vessels were installed to ride the wave of emerging brewpubs and craft breweries. In the late 1990s, a shakeout among the crop of new breweries saw some close, some absorbed by larger local operations and some surviving by remaining small.

Despite their fierce loyalty to anything local, denizens of Baltimore are also affected by the advertising and marketing clout wielded by national and international brewers. Hugh Sisson pointed out that craft breweries, like his Clipper City, account for only 3 percent of the American beer market, with imports grabbing 8 percent and big enterprises like Anheuser-Busch, In-Bev, MillerCoors and imports netting the lion's share.

In a move that might be described as faux local loyalty, or smart marketing, the makers of National Bohemian began pushing Natty Boh as Baltimore's nostalgic brew. In 2011, Pabst, which owns the rights to the beer, organized events at pubs around the city to mark the return of Natty Boh on tap. The beer, brewed in a MillerCoors facility in Eden, North Carolina, had been sold for years in cans and bottles at bargain prices. Often known as the cheapest beer to sip with steamed crabs, Natty Boh was positioning itself as a trendy brew.

Baltimore brewers predict a frothy future for better beers. They note that the big brewers have taken a page from the books of smaller craft brewers, stressing the importance of a beer's "freshness." Logic dictates that a beer brewed in Baltimore is "fresher" than one shipped from St. Louis. But logic and beer drinking are not always companions. Other factors—like income, age and family background—figure in a customer's choice of beers.

The next generation of beer drinkers gives the latest generation of Baltimore brewers hope. Baby boomers born right after World War II might have rediscovered the advantages of drinking a locally made brew. Many of the boomers' children are entering the twenty-to-forty age group, statistically the prime beer-drinking time of life. If this emerging market of beer drinkers remains loyal to the locals, the Baltimore brewing scene will flourish. If not, this city of storied beer drinkers promises to become just another pushpin on the marketing map of some distant mammoth brewery with enough advertising dollars to convert the once faithful.

Local brewers believe that once an imbiber enters the world of craft beers, there is no turning back to mainstream brews. The growth, both nationally and locally, of beer festivals and craft breweries is a sign that the brewers' optimism is warranted. If they are right, Baltimore, a city with a storied beer history, will continue to add to its rich, sudsy narrative.

Appendix

Zion Lutheran Church and the Early Baltimore Brewers

In the years before prohibition, the Baltimore brewing scene was dominated by a thicket of German families. Starting with the city's first brewer, Barnitz, and continuing through the sudsy reigns of the Bauernschmidts, the Wiessners and the Brehms, many of the city's brewers worshiped at the same church, Zion Lutheran. Sitting on Holliday Street, just east of Baltimore City Hall, the handsome brick church still has vestiges of its connection to former brewers and the brewers' largesse.

One member of the Zion congregation, Mark Duerr, has delved into the history of the brewers who attended the church. His work and synopsis of information from William J. Kelley's *Brewing in Maryland* provides clear evidence of the strong ties between the church and the city's German brewers. Moreover, his capsule descriptions of the members of the prominent brewing families—some sharing not only the same surname but also the same first name—serve as excellent guideposts in navigating the city's early brewing history.

Here is Duerr's list of the brewers who attended Zion, as well as the locations of their breweries. In addition, there are descriptions of the roles played by members of the Bauernschmidt family, one of the city's preeminent brewing clans.

Brewer and Years of Operation	Location
Elias Daniel (and father John) Barnitz, 1748–95	Hanover and Baltimore Streets
Peter Littig, 1779–89	Eastern and Central Avenues

Appendix

Brewer and Years of Operation	Location
Conrad Hoburg, 1791–96	Broadway and Fairmount Avenue
Johannes Saumenig (Camden St. Brewery), 1804–19	408 Camden Street
Henry Altvater, 1819–23	44 Clay Street (Wagon Alley)
Wehr (Herman) Hobelmann, Gottlieb and Company (Globe Brewery), 1881–88	Hanover and Conway Streets
Joshua Medtart (Saratoga Brewery), 1833–57	Fremont and Saratoga Streets
Jacob Seeger, 1854–88	Frederick and Pratt Streets
John J. Bauernschmidt Jr., 1856–79	1510 Ridgely Street
George Wiessner (Fort Marshall Brewery), 1864–99	Eastern and Highland Avenues
John F. Wiessner and Sons, 1863–1920	1700 North Gay Street
George Bauernschmidt (Greenwood Brewery), 1864–1915	1501 North Gay Street
Frank Steil (Independent Brewery), 1901–20	200 South Franklintown Road
John H. von der Horst (Eagle Brewery), 1866–1903	1900 Belair Road
August Fenker (weiss beer), 1904–19	1715 North Spring and Lanvale Streets
Henry Eigenbrot (family), 1873–1920	101–113 Willard Street
"Little" John Bauernschmidt (Mount Brewery), 1873–89	1700 Pratt Street
Frederick Bauernschmidt (American Brewery), 1900–20	Hillen and Monument Streets, Harford Road and Greenmount Avenue
John Tjarks, Monumental/Darley Park Breweries (brewery manager/investor) 1901–12	Lombard, Eaton, Haven and Baltimore Streets; Harford Road and Broadway

Appendix

Other early nineteenth-century brewers attending Zion included Johannes Delcher, Christopher Wunder, Andreas Herzog, Matthaus Muller, Johannes Beck, the Heinrich Dukehart family and Frederick Brendel. The church holds several artifacts, gifts from brewers who were once in the congregation. A plaque honoring brewer George (but spelled "Georg") Bauernschmidt is located on the north wall of the sanctuary, just inside the far right entrance. The plaque was rescued by a member of the Zion congregation after it was tossed in a dumpster during a cleaning operation. It is believed that the plaque once hung in the Eudowood Sanitarium in Towson. This facility, once located at Putty Hill and Hillen Roads, housed tuberculosis patients. The Bauernschmidt estate bequeathed $7,500 to Eudowood in 1910 with the interest from the money to fund beds at the sanitarium.

According to Kelley's book, John F. Wiessner also gave the church a small altar in 1903 to honor his parents. But records are not clear which altar it is. (John was the son of George, who originally owned the Fort Marshall Brewery, site of a former Union army Civil War fort, part of which was located at Eastern and Highland Avenues. If Confederate forces took the city, the guns of Fort Marshall were, along with guns of Fort McHenry and Fort Federal Hill, under orders to make a shambles of the city.)

The Bauernschmidt Family of Brewers

The Bauernschmidts were Baltimore's brewing dynasty. No fewer than four members of this extended family owned breweries around Baltimore before prohibition. Here is a brief description of the Bauernschmidt lineage and the breweries they operated.

John Jacob Bauernschmidt Jr.'s Lager Beer Brewery

1500 Ridgely Street, 1859–79, later Spring Garden Brewery of Bauernschmidt & Marr, 1879–89
15,000 barrels/year

John J. was born in Wambach, Bavaria, on June 10, 1830, arriving in America in 1853. John J. was the oldest and first of the brothers to come to the States. His brewery was one of the larger producers in the city during its time. As was the practice of many brewers, John's home on the brewery premises contained a large hall to house the many workers employed there.

Appendix

An on-site beer garden was advertised as Bauernschmidt's Park in the 1880s. John J. died on June 28, 1879, at age forty-nine. His widow, Elizabeth, along with her brother, John Marr, continued to operate the plant as the Spring Garden Brewery until 1889.

George Bauernschmidt's Greenwood Park Brewery

1501 North Gay Street, 1864–1915
80,000 barrels/year

George was born in Wambach, Bavaria, on May 28, 1835, arriving in Baltimore in 1853. He was the second of the three brothers to arrive in America. He married Margaretha Wiessner on September 9, 1860. Margaretha was the sister of the other Gay Street brewer, John F. Wiessner. Zion's Pastor Scheib officiated at their wedding. He also baptized all of their seven children. When George sold his brewery to the Maryland Brewing Company trust in 1899, it was the largest in Baltimore. His brands included Dancing Girl and Pilsener. He died on April 12, 1899.

John Thomas ("Little John") Bauernschmidt's Mount Brewery

1700 West Pratt Street, 1873–89
20,000 barrels/year

"Little John," the youngest of the brothers, was born in Wambach, Bavaria, on March 18, 1838, and was the third to enter the brewing business in Baltimore. He came to Baltimore in 1864. His brews were well received in the immediate area, necessitating several expansions of the brewery. In 1889, the brewery, along with two others, was purchased by the British-American Syndicate, which ran the three breweries as the City of Baltimore United Breweries, Limited. Little John died on March 3, 1897.

Fred Bauernschmidt's American Brewery

Hillen and Monument Streets, 1900–1919
400,000 barrels/year

Fred Bauernschmidt was the second son of George Bauernschmidt, owner of the Greenwood Brewery on Gay Street. Fred was born on

Appendix

January 10, 1863, and attended Scheib's School at Zion Church. On January 30, 1895, Fred was married to Agnes Wehr at Zion Church. His was the largest of Baltimore's pre-prohibition breweries in terms of annual production. The brands produced were American and Solace. A barrel sold for $4.50. Bauernschmidt bequeathed more than $5 million to local hospitals. He died on March 8, 1933, one month before repeal of prohibition. This was brewery reopened after prohibition as the Free State Brewery and later as the Wiessner Brewing Company (no relation to the pre-prohibition family of brewers).

Timeline of Significant Dates in Baltimore Brewing History

1748 John Leonard Barnitz and his son, Elias Daniel, open the city's first commercial brewery near Hanover and Baltimore Streets.

1784 Thomas Peters sets up what soon will become the young nation's largest brewery at East Lombard and the Jones Falls. Peters becomes partners with his father-in-law, Dr. Edward Johnson, who in 1808 is elected mayor and serves for the next twelve years.

1813 Mary Pickersgill is commissioned to sew a thirty- by forty-two-foot American flag. Her house is too small to hold the flag, but she gets permission from her neighbor, George Brown, now the owner of the old Peters brewery, to work there. The flag that later flies over Fort McHenry and inspires Francis Scott Key to write the national anthem was sewn in a Baltimore brewery.

1853 George Rost, a patron to many of the city's early German brewers, brings a patch of his native Bavaria, a beer garden, and his brewery, later called Standard, to Gay Street. Rost digs tunnels under his brewery to store his lager beer.

1864 George Bauernschmidt, brother of two other Bauernschmidt brewers who married into another prominent brewing clan, the Wiessners, moves his brewery from West Pratt Street to

Timeline of Significant Dates in Baltimore Brewing History

the 1500 block of North Gay Street. He bottles his own beer, and instead of hauling ice from Maine to cool his beer, he employs mechanical refrigeration. The city now supports twenty-one breweries.

1865   John von der Horst teams up with brewer Andreas Ruprechet and converts a factory on what is now the 900 block of Gay Street into the Eagle brewery. The Von der Horst family goes on to buy the Orioles baseball team, which plays in the "beer and whiskey league."

1878.   A brewery, eventually called Gunther, is formed on the south side of O'Donnell and Conkling Streets when Christian Gehl and George Gunter become partners. In 1900, Gunther's son, George Jr., forms his own Gunther brewery a few blocks away.

1885   On the north side of O'Donnell and Conkling Streets, the bankrupt brewery of Frederick and Anna Wunder is taken over by their malt suppliers. Wunder was married to another Canton brewer, Johann Baier, and remarried; she tried to keep the brewery going when her first husband died. The new owners, brothers Joseph J. and William L. Straus, work for the family's malt business. They call the new enterprise the National Brewing Company.

1887   John Frederick Wiessner erects the massive pagoda brew house on 1700 block of Gay Street. During prohibition, the building will become the American Malt Company and, after the repeal, the home of the American Brewing Company.

1899   The first beer trust, the Maryland Brewing Company, consolidates seventeen breweries into one behemoth. It will fail. In August 1901, a second beer trust, the Gottleib-Bauernschmidt-Straus Brewing Company, will consolidate the remaining breweries in the agreement. The GBS trust battles independent brewers until the start of prohibition in 1920.

1920–33   Dry times as prohibition rules the nation, although Maryland provides little state enforcement. During "the horror," Globe

Timeline of Significant Dates in Baltimore Brewing History

	makes a buzzless beer, as does Gunther. American brewery stays in business by selling malt. Globe, American, Gunther, National and Free State emerge to serve the city's post-prohibition thirst for beer.
1946	Jerry Hoffberger returns from World War II and becomes president of National Brewing Company. The company later becomes the first to package cans of beers in six-packs.
1959	Gunther brewery is sold to Theo Hamm Brewing Company of St. Paul, Minnesota.
1963	Hamm's brewery is sold to F. and M. Schaefer.
1975	The National Brewing Company merges with Carling Brewing Company, which has a modern plant on Hammonds Ferry Road and the Baltimore Beltway in Halethorpe. Brewing operations are moved to Halethorpe, and the old National plant in east Baltimore is closed in 1978. In 1979, Carling will sell the Halethorpe brewery to G. Heileman. Heileman, in turn, will sell it in 1996 to the Stroh Brewing Company, which will close the brewery that year.
1988	British Brewing Company, Maryland's first microbrewery, begins brewing beer in a Glen Burnie industrial park.
1989	Hugh Sisson opens the state's first brewpub in his family's south Baltimore tavern. In 1994, Sisson will leave the brewpub and set up Clipper City Brewing Company, which in 2010 will change the name of its line of beers to Heavy Seas.
1993	Oliver's Brewery begins making beer in the Wharf Rat Restaurant on West Pratt Street, which will become Pratt Street Ale House in 2009.
1996	Brewer's Art begins brewing Belgian beers served on draft at its North Charles Street location. In 2010, it will put its popular Resurrection Ale in cans.

Timeline of Significant Dates in Baltimore Brewing History

2006   Flying Dog starts its move from Boulder, Colorado, to Frederick, Maryland.

2012   A beer boom occurs. Monocacy Brewing Company opens a plant in Frederick. Evolution moves into a new plant in Salisbury. Union Craft Brewing plans to open in Baltimore. The ranks of craft breweries in Maryland expand to at least twenty. One of the city's vintage beers, National Premium, plans a return to the market.

Glossary of Basic Beerspeak

ABV: abbreviation of alcohol by volume, usually printed on a beer label.

adjunct: a substitute, often corn or rice, for traditional cereal grains used in the brewing recipe.

ale: one of the two basic beer types. Ales are distinguished from lagers by their use of a yeast that settles at the top of the fermentation vessel. Generally, ale yeasts prefer warmer temperatures, work quickly and yield fruity characteristics.

alt or altbier: German for "old beer," a beer made with top-fermenting yeast, such as Kolsch.

barley: the most common cereal grain used in the mash of the brewing process. Brewers use many different types of barley, kilned to different temperatures.

barrel: a standard unit of measure in brewing. In the United States, a barrel is 31.5 gallons, or about two traditional kegs.

bock : German term for a strong lager. Often but not always dark in color, bock beer can be made with wheat. The common bock beer mascot is a goat.

brewery: a facility that produces beer for sale off the premises.

Glossary of Basic Beerspeak

brewpub: a pub or tavern that produces beer on site and sells it on the premises.

craft beer: a beer produced in often limited production and using traditional methods without substituting adjuncts to lighten the flavor or the body of the beer.

draft: beer served from a cask or keg, usually unpasteurized.

growler: a vessel that holds beer, usually sixty-four ounces of draft beer. The containers are popular at brewpubs, where customers are initially charged a fee for the vessel but upon return are charged only for the beer refilling it. The origin of the name is uncertain, but it is linked to the days when neighborhood taverns sold buckets of beer. One theory is that these metal buckets "growled" as they scooted across the tavern's bar. Another is that the beer's carbonation hissed or "growled" as the bubbles pressed against the bucket lid.

hops: a flowering plants whose cones are used to give beer bitterness and aroma. Varieties of hops have different characteristics and contribute distinct flavors. The hop bitterness in a beer is measured in International Bitterness Units (IBUs), with a low number, such as 5, being mild and 100 IBUs being extreme.

lager: the second of the two basic styles of beer, lagers use yeasts that settle to the bottom of fermentation vessels. Lager yeasts prefer cooler temperatures and generally take longer to work than ale yeasts. Most mainstream American beers are light lagers.

malt: barley or other grain that has been allowed to sprout and then is dried or roasted. In many beers, the malt component is used to balance the bitterness of the hops.

pasteurization: sterilizing with heat, a process widely used in canned and bottled beers.

session beer: beer with a low alcohol content, usually 4 percent alcohol or less by volume, designed to be consumed in one sitting without becoming intoxicated.

yeast: a microorganism that during the brewing process feeds on the sugars in the solution called wort, creating alcohol and carbon dioxide. Brewers, especially those making Belgian beers, employ many yeast strains to create distinct styles and flavors.

Bibliography

Barton, Stanley. *Brewed in America*. Boston, MA: Little Brown & Company, 1962.
Berney, Louis. *Tales from the Orioles Dugout*. Champaign, IL: Sport Publishing, 2004.
Blum, Peter. *Brewed in Detroit*. Detroit, MI: Wayne State University Press, 1999.
Crouch, Andy. *Great American Craft Beer*. Philadelphia, PA: Running Press, 2010.
DeFord, Frank. *Lite Reading*. New York: Penguin Books, 1984.
Dolphin, Richard. *The International Book of Beer Can Collecting*. Secaucus, NJ: Castle Books, 1977.
Dragonwagon, Crescent. *Dairy Hollow House Soup & Bread*. New York: Workman, 1992.
Harwell, Ernie. *Ernie Harwell's Diamond Gems*. Ann Arbor, MI: Momentum Books, 1991.
Jackson, Michael. *The New World Guide to Beer*. Philadelphia, PA: Running Press, 1988.
———. *Ultimate Beer*. New York: DK Publishing, 1998.
Kelley, William J. *Brewing in Maryland*. Baltimore, MD: self-published, 1965.
Lewis, Michael J., and Charles W. Banforth. *Essays in Brewing Science*. Springer, New York, 2006.
Liebmann, George W. *Prohibition in Maryland: A Collection of Documents*. Baltimore, MD: Calvert Institute for Policy Research, 2011.
Miller, Jon, and Mark Hyman. *Confessions of a Baseball Purist*. New York: Simon & Schuster, 1998.
Mosher, Randy. *Tasting Beer*. North Adams, MA: Storey Publishing, 2009.

Bibliography

Okrent, Daniel. *Last Call: The Rise and Fall of Prohibition.* New York: Scribner, 2010.

Olesker, Michael. *The Colts' Baltimore.* Baltimore, MD: Johns Hopkins University Press, 2008.

———. *Michael Olesker's Baltimore.* Baltimore, MD: Johns Hopkins University Press, 1995.

Oliver, Garrett. *The Brewmaster's Table.* New York: HarperCollins, 2003.

Raichlen, Steven. *Beer-Can Chicken.* New York: Workman, 2002.

Rich, Laura. *Maryland History in Prints.* Baltimore, MD: Maryland Historical Society, 2002.

Schlimm, John, II. *The Ultimate Beer Lover's Cookbook.* Nashville, TN: Cumberland House, 2008.

Shields, John. *Chesapeake Bay Cooking with John Shields.* New York: Broadway Books, 1998.

Smith, Gregg. *Beer in America: The Early Years, 1587–1840: Beer's Role in the Settling of America and the Birth of the Nation.* Boulder, CO: Brewers Publications, 1998.

Smith, Gregg, and Carrie Getty. *The Beer Drinker's Bible.* Boulder, CO: Brewers Publications, 1997.

———. *Beer: A History of Suds and Civilization from Mesopotamia to Microbreweries.* New York: Avon Books, 1995.

Smith, Page. *A New Age Begins.* New York: McGraw Hill, 1976.

Steadman, John. *Days in the Sun.* Baltimore, MD: Baltimore Sun, 2000.

———. *From the Colts to the Ravens.* Centreville, MD: Tidewater Press, 1997.

Van Wieren, Dale. *American Breweries.* West Point, PA: Eastern Coast Breweriana Association, 1995.

Pamphlets Published by Baltimore Breweries and Other Periodicals

The Good Word. "Abbott and Costello Star for Gunther." December 1952. Employee magazine of Gunther Brewing Company.

———. "Baxter Ward Stars for Gunther." December 1952.

———. "Bock: The Beer of Springtime." February 1954.

———. "Colt Season Tickets Available." December 1952.

———. "Gunther Employees to Receive Free Orioles Tickets." February 1954.

———. "Gunther Scorecasters Soon to Be in Use." July 1957.

———. "Keep the (Sales) Bandwagon Rolling." March 1958.

Bibliography

———. "20,412 Tickets Pledged on Gunther Oriole TV Bandwagon Party." February 1954.

———. "Wences Wins Applause for Gunther." August 1958.

———. "We Were There, April 7, 1933." May 1958.

Gunther Brewing Company. *Designed for Wartime Living*. Baltimore, MD: self-published, undated. Recipes and games to keep spirits up during shortages imposed by World War II.

———. *The Gunther Hostess*. Baltimore, MD: self-published, undated. Recipes, many using beer, and games for home entertainment, undated.

National Brewing Company. *Brew in Your Stew*. Baltimore, MD: self-published, 1948. Recipes and adventures in the ancient, honorable and all-but-lost art of cooking with beer.

———. *Famous Maryland Recipes*. Baltimore, MD: self-published, undated. Dishes from Maryland restaurants, many now defunct, featuring local fare. Pamphlet states that National Premium was first brewed in fall of 1936.

———. *Some Old Maryland Recipes*. Baltimore, MD: self-published, 1942. Recipes featuring Maryland fare divided into four sections: seafood, beaten biscuits and breads, chicken and meat and "Maryland drinkables."

———. *When You're Going to Serve*. Baltimore, MD: self-published, undated. Pamphlet that proclaims that the ideal beverage to serve with salad is beer. Provides recipes for salad dressings.

Journals

Distelrath, Art, Jr. "American Brewing Company Baltimore, Maryland." *American Breweriana Journal* (July–August 2000).

———. "Merger Mania: The Complicated Tale of the Maryland Brewing Co. & Gottlieb-Bauernschmidt-Straus Brewing Company." *American Breweriana Journal* (January–February, 2006).

Handy, Larry. "The Arrow Beer Nudes Rare and Exotic Breweriana." *The Keg* (Winter 2006). Published by Eastern Coast Breweriana Association.

Newspapers

Jensen, Brennen. "A Beer to Call Your Own." *City Paper*, January 16, 2002.

———. "Hopping Westward." *City Paper*, May 19, 2004.

Bibliography

Kasper, Rob. "Go Micro." *Sun Magazine*, August 22, 1993. Published by the *Baltimore Sun*.

Kelly, Jacques. "Splendor Restored." *Baltimore Sun*, August 18, 2008.

Ladd, Jenn. "Ale Blazer." *City Paper*, October 5, 2011.

Maza, Erik. "Maryland Breweries Booming." *Baltimore Sun*, November 10, 2011.

Rasmussen, Frederick N. "German Thread Runs Through the City." *Baltimore Sun*, August 21, 1999.

Warren, Tim. "Microbeers: Making a Little Headway." *Sun Magazine*, February 26, 1989. Published by the *Baltimore Sun*.

Index

A

Adams, Edie 76, 77
American Brewery 21, 32, 44, 66, 69, 78, 85, 89
American Malt Company 67
Andreassen, Ray 131, 132
Arrow beer 38, 39, 62, 63, 64, 88, 93
Arrow girls 51, 63, 64
Arrow recipe book 93, 99

B

Baltimore Brewing Company 19, 114, 115, 116, 117, 129
Baltimore Colts (football) 15, 42, 46, 58, 59, 76, 81, 85, 86
Barnitz, Elias Daniel 17, 24
Barnitz, John Leonard 17, 23, 24, 39
Bauernschmidt brewery 18, 21, 32
Bauernschmidt, Frederick 21, 38, 65, 66
Bauernschmidt, George 32
Bauernschmidt, Marie 33
beeramid 106

Beer-Can Chicken 96
beer trusts 35, 38, 62, 64, 67
Benfield, David 113, 123, 124
blackbirds 91
bock beer 131, 132, 133
bottling beer 32
Brehm brewery 37, 38
Brewer's Alley 110, 124, 125
Brewer's Art 109, 118, 119, 120
Brewers Hill 14, 29, 34, 137
Brewers Row 14
Brew in Your Stew 92
British Brewing Company 17, 110, 111
broadcasters hired by breweries 84
buzzless beer 39

C

Campofreda, Nick 85
Carling-National merger 54, 111
Carneal, Herb 57, 85
Caruso, Jim 122
Cashen, Frank 14, 45, 80, 86
Clipper City Brewing Company 18, 98, 111, 113, 125, 136, 137

Index

Cohen, LeRoy "Lee" 57, 60, 61
Colt 45 52, 70, 71, 75, 76, 77, 78, 80
"Completely Unique Experience" 52, 61, 70, 75, 76, 77, 80
Costello, Bill 52, 74, 75, 76, 77, 80
crabs and beer 93, 95, 98, 137
Creegan, Tom 120
Crown Cork & Seal Company 32

D

Dairy Hollow Soup and Bread (recipe) 102
DeFord, Frank 83
DeGroen, Theo 114, 115
Demczuk, Stephen 110, 134, 135, 136
Deute, Arthur H. 21, 44, 45, 49, 91
DiPaolo, Jerome 46, 47
Distelrath, Art, Jr. 37, 38
DOG Brewing Company 129, 130
Dog Chow Cookbook 94, 100
Doner, Brod 47, 71, 73, 74, 75, 76, 80
DuClaw Brewing Company 110, 113, 123, 124

E

Ellicott Mills Brewing Company 131, 132, 133
Evolution Craft Brewing Company 110, 133

F

F. and M. Schaefer Brewing Company 62, 131
Farber, Dawson, Jr. 14, 45, 48, 52, 77, 83, 84
fishing contests 78
Fitzgerald, John J. 63
flat beer 94, 95
Flores, Tom 124, 125, 126
Flying Dog Brewery 18, 94, 98, 100, 109, 113, 120, 121, 122, 125
  name origin 122
Fordham, Benjamin 23, 24
Fordham Brewing Company 116, 126, 127
Foxx, Redd 52, 77
Frederick Brewing Company 55, 113, 121
Free State Brewery 44, 47, 60, 65, 66
Fried, Herb 71, 73
Fruchtman, JoAnn 12, 57

G

Gambrinus 67
German immigrants 15, 20, 24, 27, 28, 29, 30, 59, 66, 67, 114
Globe brewery 20, 24, 38, 39, 44, 51, 62, 63, 64, 65, 80, 93
Goss, Bailey 42, 47, 89, 90
Gottleib-Bauernschmidt-Straus Brewing Company 38, 43
growler 105, 115, 116, 117, 123, 133
Gunther Brewing Company 20, 42, 44, 46, 51, 57, 58, 60, 61, 62, 66, 73, 81, 82, 83, 85, 86, 87, 92, 105, 109, 131
Gunther, George, Jr. 37, 60
Gunther, George, Sr. 37, 59, 60

H

Hamm's bear 73, 74
Hamm's Brewing Company 61, 62, 111
Harwell, Ernie 14, 42, 57, 85
Hennessey, "Commodore" 89
Herz, Julia 93, 95

Index

Hoffberger, David 44
Hoffberger family 21, 43
Hoffberger, Jerry 22, 44, 45, 49, 54, 73, 81, 83
Hoffberger, Samuel 44, 81
Hoodle Head 130, 131
H. Straus Brothers & Company 34
Humbert, George 129, 130

I

Indian Girl 69, 78

J

Johansson's Dining House 130
Jones Falls 15, 25, 26
Jones, Stephen 117

K

Kelley, William 14, 30, 38, 51
Kessler beer 108
Knorr, Tommy 133
Kreitler, Carl 44, 48, 49
Krieger, Abraham 60
Krieger family 22, 51, 85
Krieger, Zanvyl 81, 85
Kroeger, Robert W. 47
Krueger beer can 105, 106

L

Lampart, Jay 130, 131
"Land of Pleasant Living" campaign 12, 42, 52, 70, 73, 74, 80
"Land of Sky-Blue Waters" campaign 61, 73, 75
Leonard, Captain John 64
Les Amis D'Escoffier 91

M

Maryland Brewing Company 37, 38

McDonald, Mike 127, 128
McKay, Jim 42, 47, 90
Mencken, H.L. 39
Merzbacher, John, Sr. 66
Miss Beer Can 107
Monocacy Brewing Company 110, 124, 125, 126
Monroe, Marilyn 51, 64
Monumental Brewing Company 21, 40, 41
Mr. Boh 45, 46, 52, 55
Mug Club 115, 116
Murray, Jane Ward 69, 78

N

National Bohemian 18, 34, 42, 48, 49, 52, 54, 70, 75, 80, 87, 90, 106, 113, 137
National Brewing Company 20, 34, 38, 41, 42, 51, 52, 53, 54, 74, 76, 81, 83, 84, 85, 86, 90, 91, 92, 105, 109, 134, 137
National Premium 13, 18, 34, 42, 48, 49, 51, 54, 56, 91, 113, 121
North German Lloyd Steamship Company 27

O

Oliver, Bill 116, 117, 118
Oliver Breweries 116
Orioles baseball 34, 45, 59, 81, 83, 84, 86, 88, 90, 115
Owens, Hamilton 66

P

Peters brewery 25
Pickersgill, Mary 15, 25, 114
Poe, Edgar Allan 135
Powell, John ""Boog 82, 86, 87
Pratt Street Ale House 117, 118

Index

prohibition 27, 35, 38, 39, 41, 43, 48, 60, 62, 63, 64, 65, 66, 67, 105, 116

R

Rams Head 126
Raven Special Lager 110, 135
Red Brick Station 109, 127
Resurrection Ale 19, 119, 120
Rizzuto, Phil 57, 85
Rost brewery 30, 34
Rost, George 29
Ruppert, Colonel Jacob 60

S

Sandler, Gilbert 33, 73
Sarubin, Morton 66
Schaefer, William Donald 55
Schnably, Don 12, 75
Schuetzenfest 31
scoreboards 59, 81, 82, 87, 88
scorecasters 59
Señor Wences 58
Shields, John 94, 95
shire horses 51
Sisson brewpub 111
Sisson, Hugh 17, 98, 110, 111, 112, 113, 114, 116, 117, 125, 129, 137
Stewart, Volker 120
Stillwater Artisanal Ales 134
Stranahan, George 122
Straus brothers, Henry and Levy 34
Straus brothers, Joseph and William 34
Strumke, Brian 134, 135

T

Tewey, Mark 112, 113, 121, 123
The Gunther Hostess Book 92, 96, 97, 100
The Laughing Cavalier 64, 80
"The Star-Spangled Banner" 15, 25, 135
Thompson, Chuck 14, 84, 85
Trabert, "Turkey" Joe 14, 85, 88, 103

U

Union Craft Brewing 109

V

Van, Billy 70, 71, 75, 77, 78, 80
Von der Horst Brewing Company 38, 81
Von der Horst, Henry 34
Von der Horst, John 34

W

W.B. Doner ad agency 71
White Marsh Brewing Company 127
Wiessner, John F. 21, 28, 66, 67
World War II 44, 51, 60, 91, 92, 105, 138

Y

Yuengling, David Gottlieb 29

Z

Zion Lutheran Church 20, 24, 27

About the Author and Photographer

Jim Burger has been a professional photographer for more than twenty-five years. Since his earliest days, developing pictures in his parents' basement, he has used a camera to tell stories. He learned his craft at the Maryland Institute College of Art, and he learned his trade at the *Baltimore City Paper* and the *Baltimore Sun*. As a freelance photographer, he has taken a personal approach to any assignment. His work has appeared in the *Philadelphia Inquirer*, the *San Francisco Examiner* and the *Los Angeles Times*, and he has worked for clients as varied as AARP, Blue Cross/Blue Shield and the Lou Gehrig's Disease Association. The son of a Pittsburgh-area tavern owner, he has a longstanding interest in brewery artifacts and has decorated his Baltimore row home with prime examples of brewery art.

About the Author and Photographer

Rob Kasper is a Baltimore writer. For more than three decades, he was a reporter, columnist and editorial writer for the *Baltimore Sun*, often writing about the area's food and drink. In the fall of 2011, he left the newspaper to finish writing this book.

He has won numerous writing awards. The Association of Food Journalists cited his 2008 food columns as among the best in American and Canadian newspapers. This marked the fifth time in two decades that his writing has been so honored by the association. He has also won two National Headliner Awards. His interest in local history and Baltimore brewers led him in 2009 to become a founding member of Baltimore Beer Week, a not-for-profit organization that celebrates the area's brewing culture.

A native of Dodge City, Kansas, he received his undergraduate degree in American studies from the University of Kansas and a master of science in journalism from Northwestern University, graduating with honors and distinction. He was a reporter for the *Hammond (IN) Times* and the *Louisville Times* newspapers before joining the *Sun*. He lives with his wife, Judith, a professor in the Johns Hopkins Bloomberg School of Public Health, in a downtown Baltimore row house. They have two sons.

www.ingramcontent.com/pod-product-compliance
Lightning Source LLC
Chambersburg PA
CBHW070344100426
42812CB00005B/1416